THE EASY BIRD GUIDE

Western Region

A Quick Identification Guide
for All Birders

John Bull and Edith Bull

Illustrated by James Coe

FALCONGUIDE®

GUILFORD, CONNECTICUT
HELENA, MONTANA

AN IMPRINT OF THE GLOBE PEQUOT PRESS

Falcon and FalconGuide are registered trademarks of Morris Book Publishing, LLC.

Map by M.A. Dubé © Morris Book Publishing, LLC.

Library of Congress Cataloging-in-Publication Data
Bull, John L.
  The easy bird guide. Western region : a quick identification guide for
all birders / by John Bull and Edith Bull ; illustrated by James Coe.-- 1st ed.
    p. cm.
  Includes index.
  ISBN 0-7627-3742-5
  1. Birds--West (U.S.)--Identification. I. Bull, Edith. II. Prall,
Pieter D. III. Title.
  QL683.W4B852 2006
  598.0978--dc22
                                              2005027248

Printed in China
First Globe Pequot Edition/First Printing

The authors and The Globe Pequot Press assume no liability for accidents happening to, or injuries sustained by, readers who engage in the activities described in this book.

gments

T his book is the product of our collective years of working, teaching, and volunteering at major natural history museums and nature organizations; of leading field trips and lecturing about birds; and of writing about birds for professionals, the media, and the public. We realized that the beginning birder needed easy-to-understand information about birding. The result is this book, which aims to help the uninitiated learn about birds quickly and easily, and to serve as a teaching tool for beginning bird-watchers.

When we conceived the idea of our book, which was originally published as a Macmillan Field Guide in 1989, we wrote it for baby-boomers during the mass exodus of educated and environmentally aware people from the cities and suburbia to the countryside in the mid- to late 1980s. Today we envision those weathering baby-boomers using this new edition to teach their grandchildren about birds during the 2000s.

There are several people we would like to thank for their suggestions and contributions. Guy Tudor and John Yrizarry offered many helpful ideas about the comparative plates in the illustrated section of this book. We are also greatly indebted to the staff at the Department of Ornithology at the American Museum of Natural History. Their contributions are greatly appreciated. We would also like to thank Laura Strom and Jan Cronan of The Globe Pequot Press for their enthusiastic support of this project, and Lori Andiman for her unswerving dedication and valuable time and effort that helped bring this book to press. James Coe would like to thank his family for their encouragement and unwavering support.

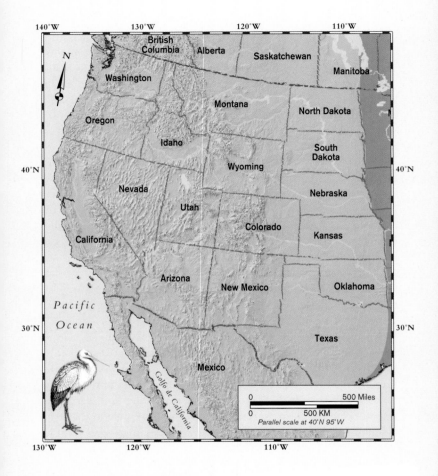

Contents

Introduction

T his book is intended to teach the beginner about easily identifying birds. It has a unique format that will help even novices learn to recognize species quickly.

How to Use This Guide

Rather than present birds in scientific categories, we group them according to similarity of color, pattern, behavior, or habitat. We have, for example, Reddish Birds, Bluish Birds, Tree Clingers, Woodpeckers, Flycatchers, Swallows, Grassland Birds, and Large Shorebirds. The text accompanying each color plate—indeed, each species—emphasizes simply and quickly the salient features, the so-called field marks, that enable you to sort out a particular bird almost instantly. You will find that certain field marks appear in italics—these are the critical distinguishing marks of particular species.

For easy reference we have also arranged the birds according to their abundance. Most bird guides follow a strict phylogenetic, or evolutionary, order in presenting the birds, beginning with the supposedly most primitive types—the loons and grebes—and ending with the most advanced—the finches and sparrows. In other words, they start with the waterbirds and finish with the land birds. In this volume, we reverse the sequence, starting with the more familiar land birds of yard, garden, field, and park, such as the blackbirds, sparrows, thrushes, and warblers. We end with the somewhat less familiar aquatic types, such as the ducks, gulls, and herons.

Further, to minimize confusion, we have chosen to focus on the most common and conspicuous species rather than on the 700 or so that are found in the western United States. There are 340 species illustrated in the 54 plates. Some of the birds included are common throughout the West, some in specific regions of the West, others in rather small areas of the West. No rare birds are depicted, but some species are uncommon in various regions, while abundant elsewhere. The Greater Roadrunner, for example, is commonly seen in parts of the Southwest, especially Arizona, but rarely ventures as far northeast as Kansas. For our purposes western North America stretches from southern Canada (50°N) to the Mexican border and from the Pacific coast to the Dakotas and the southernmost Gulf coast of Texas (see map). The dividing line begins on the eastern borders of North and South Dakota, Nebraska, Kansas, and Oklahoma and includes most of Texas, excepting much of the southeastern portion.

Beginning Birding

The easiest way to begin birding is to look out of your window. If you live in the suburbs, you know that there are always birds around, even if you haven't been able to identify them. In the city, you have certainly seen pigeons, European Starlings, and House Sparrows.

Read the entire book and browse through the plates to familiarize yourself with the general information and with the overall appearance of various birds. Then keep this book handy—in the kitchen, where you may look out the window, see a bird alight on the patio, and wonder what it is; in your pocket, purse, or briefcase for those times when you are strolling through the park or walking to work, or along the beach; and in your car for those trips on which keeping an eye on the local birds can add greatly to the fun of a vacation.

Humans have the urge to name things; we feel that somehow we have gotten a grasp on reality or have penetrated to the essence of a thing if we can attach a name to it. One of the satisfactions of birding is being able to name the birds we see, thereby establishing some kind of mastery over the natural wonders that surround us, even in the densest urban locality.

It's not hard to become a reasonably perceptive birder. Start by identifying those birds you see repeatedly around your home. Learn without any possibility of doubt to recognize the House Sparrow, Northern Cardinal, or Mourning Dove. Once you've mastered these birds—and it won't take long—your eye and brain will be sure to recognize that something that flew by was *not* one of those. There lies the road to advanced birding, and, one hopes, the urge to wander farther afield—to the pond, marsh, wooded estate, beach, lake, or sanctuary.

Without being exhaustive or exhausting, this guide will also tell you what *not* to look for and where and when *not* to look for it, for the process of elimination is an important factor in identification. Although in birding, as in most activities, there are exceptions to every rule, you don't really have to worry about the exceptions.

The "not" factor is important in eliminating things you don't have to worry about. To give just one far-fetched example, remember the Ancient Mariner and his albatross? Why an Albatross? Because he was a seaman, and albatrosses are found only over the oceans. Therefore, a big bird sitting in a tree in your yard will definitely not be an albatross. You can, with impunity, rule that out, without knowing anything else about the bird in your tree.

The elimination process also operates by seasons. Many birds are migratory and spend various seasons in various places. Thus, flycatchers, vireos, and warblers, which are insect-eating birds, will not be found in the northern latitudes in winter, for there is no food for them.

Organization of the Plates

The color plates, in most instances, group birds according to their appearance, even when the birds are not taxonomically related. The fact is that many birds, though widely separated by evolution, often look remarkably alike, especially to the novice. We call them "unrelated look-alikes."

To keep the book as straightforward as possible, we show the outstanding colors and patterns for each species. When males and females differ greatly in appearance, both are shown, or the differences are mentioned in the text opposite the plate. Males *usually* have more distinctive plumage than females, both as to color and pattern, so we have depicted more males. On Plate 26, for example, we show eight male hummingbirds with outstanding markings. Their female counterparts are somewhat drab and, if depicted, would look confusingly similar. So, only one female, the Black-chinned Hummingbird—a common and widespread species—is shown in flight, hovering in front of a flower.

In other cases—for example, among the vast number of waterbirds—the sexes are virtually identical or similar in plumage. For these birds, only one figure per species is illustrated.

Explanation of the Plates

The bird world is divided into waterbirds and land birds, although many of each are often found in the other's habitat.

Waterbirds include swans, geese, ducks, and other ducklike birds, generally described as waterfowl. Waterbirds also include such wading birds as herons and egrets. Finally, waterbirds encompass shore-birds, such as plovers and sandpipers, gulls and terns.

The land birds take in everything else—the birds we see in woods, fields, yards, gardens, parks, farms, villages, and city streets: the hawks, owls, pigeons, sparrows, woodpeckers, warblers, finches, and so on.

We have tried to depict birds in natural positions and settings, while emphasizing their distinguishing markings. For example, most waterfowl are shown only in the water or when they are perched. Flying birds are kept to a minimum—most ducks are more difficult to identify in flight. Certain exceptions include the Willet, which reveals its distinctive black-and-white wing pattern only while in flight, not when at rest. Hawks, by contrast, *are* depicted in flight, to emphasize their distinctive underwing markings and because their body and tail patterns, their shape, and their flight behavior are important factors in identification.

To keep bird identification as easy as possible, the descriptions opposite each plate have been pared to the absolute essentials. You will find that many of the details in the paintings are not mentioned in the descriptive material opposite the plates. The text highlights only those field marks that distinguish a particular bird from all others.

No attempt is made to describe bird songs, but for those few whose call is familiar, that fact is mentioned.

The plates that follow may be used without further comments, except one: You do need to know roughly what group of birds you're looking for. Is your bird a duck or a gull? A finch or a warbler? The "Further Comments on the Plates" chapter provides added informa-tion about these groupings, making it easier to use the plates.

You may say that of course you know the difference between a duck and a gull. Fine, that's a good start. But what about the differ-ence between a duck and a goose? A bluebird and a Blue Jay? Or a Blue Jay and a kingfisher? Knowing such differences—or at least appreciating the fact that they exist—is the first step to identifying what you see.

For example: The Belted Kingfisher is always found near water, for it feeds only on small fish; you will not find this bird in the mid-dle of a forest or in a desert or anywhere far from water. It has a very large, shaggy head, which makes it look top-heavy. It is possible, however, for the beginner to confuse it with the Blue Jay, because both birds have a generally blue-white appearance and both have crests. But the Blue Jay's head does not have that outsized appearance, and the Blue Jay is smaller than the Belted Kingfisher. Further, the Belted Kingfisher dives into the water for its food, something the Blue Jay never does.

Take another example—obvious, perhaps, but basic: Most ducks don't roost in trees; they are usually (although not always) found on the ground or in the water. So, if you saw a rather large bird perched in a tree, the chances are good that it wouldn't be a duck. This is identification by elimination. Identification is made easier by knowing immediately what a bird cannot be.

Before you do any birding, we suggest that you read the material opposite the plates. It will simplify the process of learning to identify birds. There is also much additional information in the "Further Comments on the Plates" chapter.

Plate Key

Descriptions

M. = male
F. = female
imm. = immature
juv. = juvenile

Plumage Phases

dark phase
light phase
blue phase
white phase

Seasons

summer
winter

Locations

c. = central
e. = eastern
e.c. = east central
n. = northern
n.c. = north central
n.e. = northeastern
n.w. = northwestern
s. = southern
s.c. = south central
s.e. = southeastern
s.w. = southwestern
w. = western
w.c. = west central
U.S. = United States

Identifying Birds by Field Marks

On the following pages you will find black-and-white figures describing bird topography or field marks, as well as some examples of wings, tails, bills, and feet. These physical features—and others, such as crests and the various patterns and colors of the plumage—form what are known as field marks. The following summary of the black-and-white illustrations contains an example of each type of anatomical feature.

Familiarize yourself with the examples illustrated and you will find that learning to distinguish the different birds will soon become a relatively easy and fascinating pastime.

Facing each color plate is the description of the bird shown, enabling the reader to identify it. All the important characteristics of size, shape, color, pattern, and—where relevant—behavior are indicated. No irrelevant or confusing detailed descriptions are included.

Following the section on field marks are two categories:

1. **Habitat**—Only those places are mentioned in which the bird may be found during the nesting season—usually in spring and summer or, if relevant, in fall and winter. Spring and fall migrations are normally excluded, since birds may turn up in many different habitats at those times. However, if the bird in question is found only during spring and/or fall, then the habitats are listed.

2. **Range**—It is most important for the observer to know *where* a bird is likely to occur. The map shows the area covered in this volume. For example, a few species live in a very restricted area, such as in the southern portion of Texas, Arizona, or California. At the other extreme, a large percentage of the birds included in this book are widespread in range, and this information is given—for example, "from s. Canada to the Mexican border."

Field Marks (Body Characteristics)

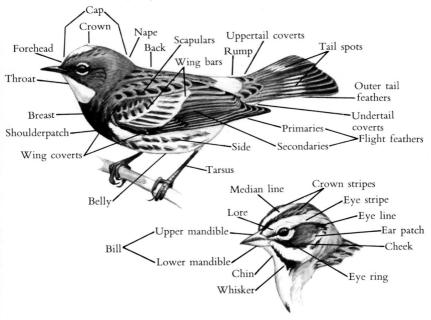

Cap
Crown
Nape
Scapulars
Uppertail coverts
Tail spots
Forehead
Back
Rump
Wing bars
Throat
Breast
Shoulderpatch
Wing coverts
Side
Primaries
Secondaries
Undertail coverts
Flight feathers
Outer tail feathers
Tarsus
Belly

Median line
Crown stripes
Eye stripe
Eye line
Lore
Ear patch
Upper mandible
Cheek
Bill
Lower mandible
Eye ring
Chin
Whisker

Wing Shapes

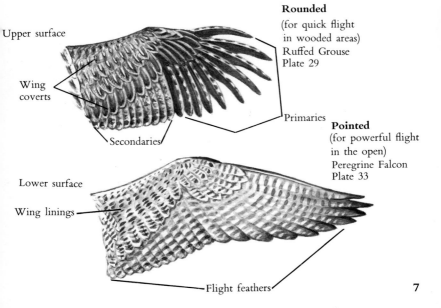

Upper surface

Wing coverts

Secondaries

Rounded
(for quick flight
in wooded areas)
Ruffed Grouse
Plate 29

Primaries

Pointed
(for powerful flight
in the open)
Peregrine Falcon
Plate 33

Lower surface

Wing linings

Flight feathers

7

Tail Shapes

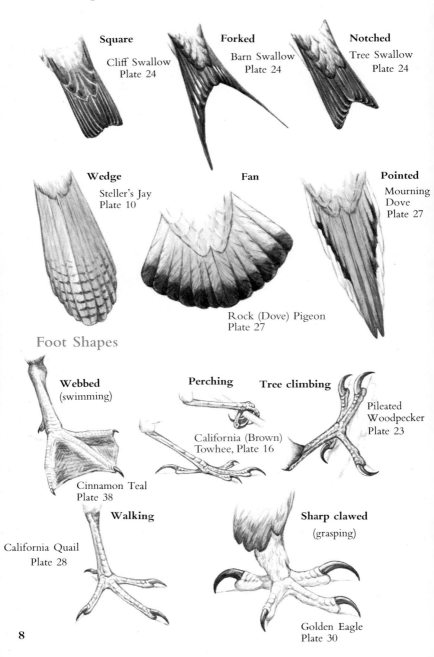

Square

Cliff Swallow
Plate 24

Forked

Barn Swallow
Plate 24

Notched

Tree Swallow
Plate 24

Wedge

Steller's Jay
Plate 10

Fan

Pointed

Mourning
Dove
Plate 27

Rock (Dove) Pigeon
Plate 27

Foot Shapes

Webbed
(swimming)

Perching

Tree climbing

Pileated
Woodpecker
Plate 23

California (Brown)
Towhee, Plate 16

Cinnamon Teal
Plate 38

Walking

Sharp clawed
(grasping)

California Quail
Plate 28

Golden Eagle
Plate 30

Bill Shapes

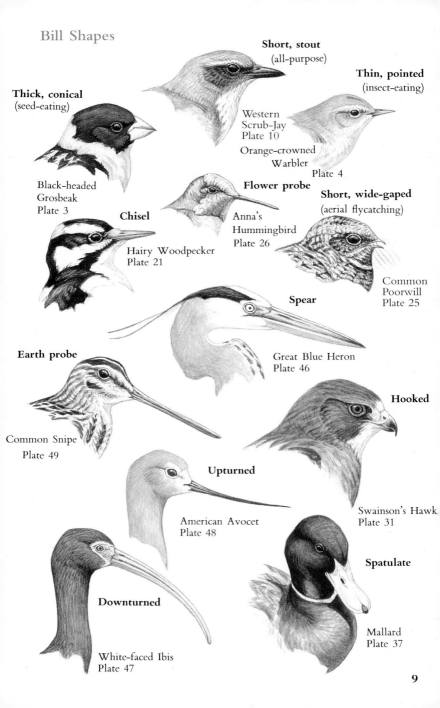

Short, stout
(all-purpose)

Western
Scrub-Jay
Plate 10

Thin, pointed
(insect-eating)

Orange-crowned
Warbler
Plate 4

Thick, conical
(seed-eating)

Black-headed
Grosbeak
Plate 3

Flower probe

Anna's
Hummingbird
Plate 26

Short, wide-gaped
(aerial flycatching)

Chisel

Hairy Woodpecker
Plate 21

Common
Poorwill
Plate 25

Spear

Great Blue Heron
Plate 46

Earth probe

Common Snipe
Plate 49

Hooked

Upturned

American Avocet
Plate 48

Swainson's Hawk
Plate 31

Spatulate

Downturned

White-faced Ibis
Plate 47

Mallard
Plate 37

Plate 1. **REDDISH BIRDS**

PURPLE FINCH 6"

Washed with purplish red; *unstreaked sides;* female—heavily streaked brown; white line behind eye; dark face patches. **Habitat:** Conifers, mixed woods; orchards, gardens, parks, yards; feeders. **Range:** Mainly Pacific Coast from s. Canada to Mexican border.

HOUSE FINCH 5½"

Red forehead, eye line, throat, breast, and rump; *streaked sides;* whitish wing bars; female—heavily streaked brown; no facial pattern. **Habitat:** Conifers, mixed woods; dry scrub; ranches, farms; parks, suburbs, cities; feeders. **Range:** S. British Columbia to Mexican border, east throughout most of U.S.

WHITE-WINGED CROSSBILL 6½"

Bright pink; black tail and wings; two white wing bars; crossed bill at close range. **Habitat:** Conifers; winter—also mixed woods. **Range:** S. British Columbia, Alberta to Washington, Montana, n.w. Wyoming; in winter to Oregon, Utah, n. New Mexico.

RED CROSSBILL 6"

Brick red; blackish wings and tail; crossed bill at close range. **Habitat:** Conifers; winter—also mixed woods. **Range:** S. British Columbia, Alberta to Mexican border at higher elevations, east to edge of Great Plains; winters to n.w. Texas.

PINE GROSBEAK 9"

Pinkish red with gray sides and belly; blackish tail and wings; two white wing bars. **Habitat:** Conifers; winter—also mixed woods; orchards. **Range:** S. British Columbia, s.w. Alberta to mountains of c. California, n. Arizona, New Mexico; winters to n.w. Texas, n. Oklahoma.

GRAY-CROWNED ROSY-FINCH 6"

Black forehead; gray hind-crown; brown cheeks, back, throat, and breast; pinkish rose rump, sides, and belly; pinkish wash on wings; yellow bill in winter. **Habitat:** High altitudes above tree line on bare ground and rocks, in short grass; winter—at lower elevations, mainly grassy fields, but often at feeders in severe weather. **Range:** Mountains from s. British Columbia, Alberta to c. California, n. Arizona, New Mexico; winters from w. portions of Dakotas to Kansas.

10

Plate 1. **REDDISH BIRDS**

Purple Finch
F.
M.

F.
M.
House Finch

White-winged Crossbill

Red Crossbill

Pine Grosbeak

Gray-crowned Rosy-Finch

11

Plate 2. **REDDISH/ORANGE BIRDS**

BULLOCK'S ORIOLE 7½"

Black and bright orange; large white wing patch; black tail with orange patches; female—greenish gray back; yellowish head and throat; grayish white belly. **Habitat:** Open woods, river groves, roadside shade trees; farms, towns; occasionally at feeders. **Range:** S. Canada to Mexican border, east to edge of Great Plains; winters south of border.

HOODED ORIOLE 7½"

Black and bright orange; orange crown and head; black face, throat, and chest; *all*-black tail. **Habitat:** Riverine trees, especially palms, willows, cottonwoods; scrub in arid areas; city parks, suburban hummingbird feeders. **Range:** C. portions of California, Nevada south to Mexican border, southeast to s. Texas; winters north to s. Arizona.

VERMILION FLYCATCHER 6"

Flaming red crown and underparts; blackish brown above. **Habitat:** Arid areas with scattered trees and shrubs near ponds and streams. **Range:** S. California, Arizona, New Mexico, w. and s. Texas; winters to just north of Mexican border.

SUMMER TANAGER 7½"

Rose-red; *pale* bill. **Habitat:** Cottonwoods and willows along streams and near ponds. **Range:** S.w. U.S. north and east to c. California, s. Nevada, Utah, Texas, c. Oklahoma; winters south of Mexican border.

HEPATIC TANAGER 7½"

Brick red; grayish cheeks, *dark* bill. **Habitat:** Mixed pine-oak forests at higher elevations. **Range:** S. California, Arizona, New Mexico, w. Texas; winters mainly south of Mexican border.

PYRRHULOXIA 8"

Gray with dark red crest, face, outer wings, and tail; rose-pink below from throat to center of belly; *yellow* bill. **Habitat:** Generally, dry open country with thickets, thorn scrub, hedgerows; ranches; feeders. **Range:** S. parts of Arizona, New Mexico; w. and s.c. Texas.

NORTHERN CARDINAL 8½"

Bright *red,* including crest and bill; *black* face; female—similar, but light brown; only bill, tip of crest, wings, and tail are *red.* **Habitat:** Wooded edges, thickets, hedges; city parks, suburban gardens, yards; feeders; also desert scrub. **Range:** S.e. South Dakota south through Great Plains states to w. and s. Texas; s.w. U.S. from s. parts of New Mexico, Arizona to s. California (local).

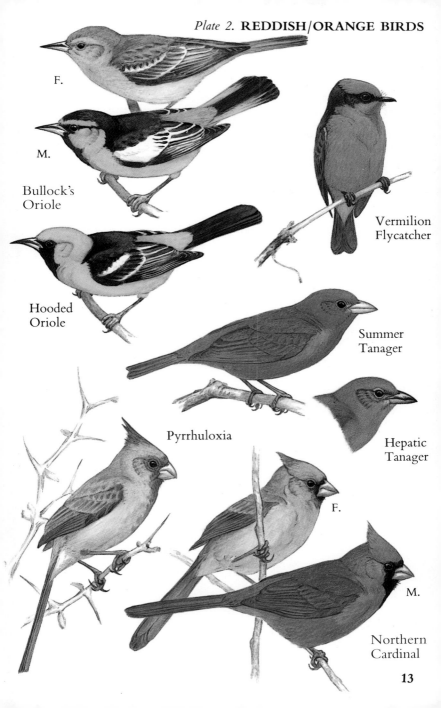

Plate 2. **REDDISH/ORANGE BIRDS**

F.

M.

Bullock's
Oriole

Hooded
Oriole

Vermilion
Flycatcher

Summer
Tanager

Pyrrhuloxia

Hepatic
Tanager

F.

M.

Northern
Cardinal

13

Plate 3. **YELLOWISH BIRDS**

LESSER (GREEN-BACKED) GOLDFINCH 4"

Black crown, tail, and wings; white wing patch; green nape, back, and rump; yellow below; Black-backed form similar, but all black above. **Habitat:** Open brushy fields, wooded edges; farms, gardens; suburban feeders. **Range:** W. Oregon, California east to Colorado, New Mexico, s.w. Texas. "Green-backed" form occurs in w. parts, "Black-backed" in e. parts; rare in winter north to Utah, Colorado.

LAWRENCE'S GOLDFINCH 4¼"

Black face, tail, and wings; *three* yellow wing patches; gray hindcrown cheeks, back, and flanks; yellow rump and breast. **Habitat:** Dry, grassy hillsides; canyons with scattered trees and shrubs; fields; suburban feeders. **Range:** Local from n. California, c. Arizona to Mexican border.

PINE SISKIN 5"

Heavily streaked; slender bill; small yellow patches on wings and tail. **Habitat:** Conifers in summer, bushy fields in winter; feeders. **Range:** Canada to Mexican border but erratic and irregular in winter in South.

AMERICAN GOLDFINCH 5"

Bright yellow body; black forecrown, wings, and tail; female—mostly olive above, dull yellow below; black wings and tail. **Habitat:** Weedy fields; farms, orchards, gardens; city parks; suburban feeders. **Range:** S. Canada to Mexican border; in winter withdraws from n. portions.

SCOTT'S ORIOLE 8"

Black head, throat, breast, upper back, and tail; yellow rump, belly, bend of wing, and sides of tail. **Habitat:** Arid areas with yuccas, palms, pinyon-oak woods; occasionally at hummingbird feeders. **Range:** C. California, Nevada, Utah to Mexican border, s.e. to w. Texas; some winter in s. California, s.e. Arizona.

WESTERN TANAGER 7"

Red head; black back, wings, and tail; yellow body; two wing bars— one yellow, one white. **Habitat:** Montane conifer forests in summer; migration—lowland deciduous woods and fruit trees. **Range:** S. British Columbia, Alberta to Mexican border, east to edge of Great Plains; winters south of border.

BLACK-HEADED GROSBEAK 7½"

Black head, back, tail, and wings; two white wing bars; orange-brown collar, rump, breast, and sides; yellow belly. **Habitat:** Open mixed forests, wooded edges. **Range:** S. British Columbia, Alberta to Mexican border, east to Dakotas, Nebraska, Kansas; winters south of border.

EVENING GROSBEAK 8"

Golden yellow and dark brown; yellow forecrown and eye line; black tail and wings; large white wing patch; thick yellowish bill. **Habitat:** Conifers, mixed forests in summer; shade trees, city parks; suburban feeders. **Range:** S. British Columbia, Alberta to Mexican border, local in Southwest.

Lesser (Green-backed) Goldfinch

Plate 3. **YELLOWISH BIRDS**

Lawrence's Goldfinch

Pine Siskin

F.

M.

American Goldfinch

Scott's Oriole

Western Tanager

Black-headed Grosbeak

Evening Grosbeak

15

Plate 4. **YELLOWISH WARBLERS**

VIRGINIA'S WARBLER 4½"

Gray above; yellow rump; white eye ring; white below; yellow breast and vent; close range—rufous crown patch. **Habitat:** Montane areas with brush, pinyon-juniper woodland; yellow pine, spruce, fir. **Range:** E. Nevada, Utah, w. Colorado to s.e. California, Arizona, s.w. New Mexico, extreme w. Texas; winters south of border.

LUCY'S WARBLER 4"

Gray above; rufous crown patch, rump; white below. **Habitat:** Desert mesquite; willows, cottonwoods along streams. **Range:** Mexican border to California, Nevada, Utah, Arizona, New Mexico; winters south of border.

NASHVILLE WARBLER 4½"

Gray head; white eye ring; yellow below. **Habitat:** Open mixed woods; damp thickets; spruce-sphagnum bogs; parks, yards. **Range:** S. British Columbia, s.e. Manitoba; Washington, Idaho, w. Montana to c. California, Nevada, Utah; winters in s. California (local) and south of border.

ORANGE-CROWNED WARBLER 5"

Olive greenish above, drab yellowish below; grayish breast streaks close-up; "orange" crown patch often hidden. **Habitat:** Brushy clearings; aspen, willow thickets; fields at forest borders. **Range:** S. Canada and U.S. from Pacific Coast east along Rockies to Mexican border; winters north to Oregon coast, inland to California, Arizona, s. Texas.

YELLOW WARBLER 5"

Yellow, including wing bars; red breast streaks (male). **Habitat:** Willows, alders along streams; orchards, gardens, parks. **Range:** S. Canada to Mexican border; winters south of border, north to s. California, Arizona.

WILSON'S WARBLER 5"

Black cap; yellow face and below. **Habitat:** Moist thickets, woodlands; gardens, parks, yards. **Range:** S. parts of British Columbia, Alberta, Washington, Idaho, w. Montana, in mountains to s. California, local to s. Arizona, New Mexico; winters south of border.

COMMON YELLOWTHROAT 5"

Black mask; yellow throat and breast; female—lacks mask. **Habitat:** Moist thickets, marshes, fields; parks, gardens. **Range:** S. Canada to Mexican border; winters north to California, east to c. Texas.

MACGILLIVRAY'S WARBLER 5¼"

Gray hood; black chest; partial white eye ring; yellow breast, belly. **Habitat:** Damp, shady thickets. **Range:** S. British Columbia, Alberta to c. California, east to mountains to w. New Mexico; winters south of border.

YELLOW-BREASTED CHAT 7½"

Our largest warbler—dark olive-green above, white spectacles; yellow throat, breast; white belly. **Habitat:** Dense thickets, briers. **Range:** S. Canada to Mexican border; winters south of border, north to Texas.

Plate 4. **YELLOWISH WARBLERS**

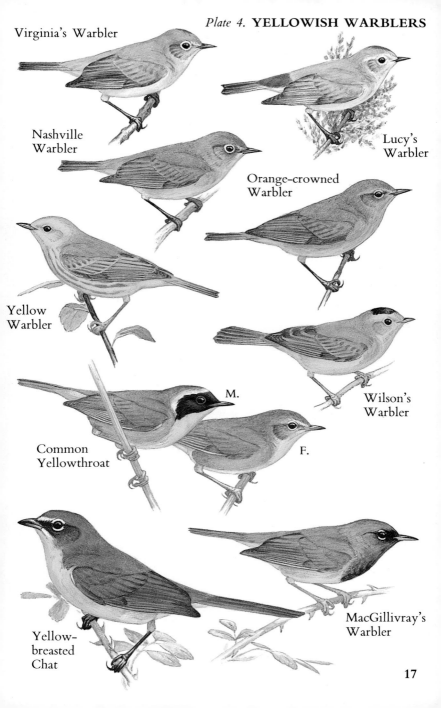

Virginia's Warbler

Lucy's Warbler

Nashville Warbler

Orange-crowned Warbler

Yellow Warbler

Wilson's Warbler

Common Yellowthroat

M.

F.

Yellow-breasted Chat

MacGillivray's Warbler

17

Plate 5. **OTHER WARBLERS**

HERMIT WARBLER 4½"

Yellow face, black throat; gray back, tail, wings; two white wing bars; white breast, belly. **Habitat:** Montane conifer forests; migration—hardwoods. **Range:** Pacific Coast, interior mountains of s.w. Washington, Oregon, California; winters south of border, rarely to c. California.

GRACE'S WARBLER 5"

Gray above; two white wing bars; yellow and white eye line; yellow throat and breast, white belly; black streaks along sides. **Habitat:** Montane pine, oak forests. **Range:** S. parts of Nevada, Utah, Colorado to Mexican border of Arizona, New Mexico; also extreme w. Texas; winters south of border.

TOWNSEND'S WARBLER 5"

Black crown, cheek, throat; yellow line over and under cheek; yellow breast, black side stripes; two white wing bars. **Habitat:** Conifer forests; migration/winter—hardwoods. **Range:** S. British Columbia to Oregon, Idaho, c. Montana, w. Wyoming; migrates east to Great Plains; winters on coast of s. Oregon, California, and south of Mexican border.

BLACK-THROATED GRAY WARBLER 5"

Like Townsend's Warbler, but yellow replaced by white. **Habitat:** Deciduous, mixed woods. **Range:** S. British Columbia, Idaho, Wyoming to Mexican border; winters north to s. California, s.w. Arizona.

YELLOW-RUMPED (AUDUBON'S RACE) WARBLER 5¼"

Yellow rump, crown, throat, sides; black face and chest; gray back, tail, wings; white wing patch, breast, and belly; fall/winter—much duller, more brownish. **Habitat:** Conifer forests; migration/winter—mixed woodlands, thickets, gardens, parks. **Range:** S. Canada to Mexican border winters north, coast lowlands to British Columbia, inland to s.w. United States.

AMERICAN REDSTART 5"

Black head and body; orange wing and tail patches; white belly; female—like male but with yellow patches; olive above, white below; gray head. **Habitat:** Open woodland; trees, shrubs. **Range:** s. Canada to Washington, Idaho, Utah, Colorado, e. Oklahoma; winters south of border, north to s. Texas.

RED-FACED WARBLER 5¼"

Scarlet face, throat, and chest; black cap and cheeks; white nape, rump, breast, and belly; gray back, wings, and tail. **Habitat:** Mountain forests. **Range:** North to e. Arizona, s.w. New Mexico; winters south of border.

PAINTED REDSTART 5¼"

Black with scarlet breast; white wing and tail patches. **Habitat:** Montane hardwoods, especially oak; pine—often in canyons. **Range:** North to c. Arizona, s.w. New Mexico, w. Texas (Chisos Mountains); winters south of border, rarely in s. Arizona. **Note:** Both redstarts flit about with spread wings and tail; frequently flycatching.

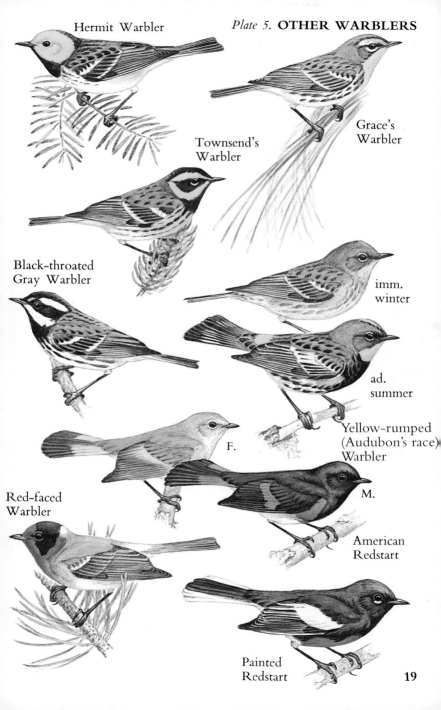

Hermit Warbler

Plate 5. **OTHER WARBLERS**

Grace's Warbler

Townsend's Warbler

Black-throated Gray Warbler

imm. winter

ad. summer

Yellow-rumped (Audubon's race) Warbler

F.

M.

Red-faced Warbler

American Redstart

Painted Redstart

19

Plate 6. **GREENISH/GRAYISH BIRDS**
(Kinglets, Vireos)

RUBY-CROWNED KINGLET 4¼"

Tiny, short-tailed; white eye ring and wing bars; red crown patch (male only); olive above, grayish below. **Habitat:** Summer—conifers; migration/winter—mixed woodlands, thickets, shrubs. **Range:** S. British Columbia, Alberta, w. Montana through mountains to Mexican border; winters north to Oregon.

GOLDEN-CROWNED KINGLET 4"

Tiny, short tailed; black–and–white eye stripes; white wing bars; crown orange (male), yellow (female); olive above, grayish below. **Habitat:** Summer-conifers; migration/winter—mixed woodlands, thickets, shrubs. **Range:** S. Canada through mountains to Mexican border.

GRAY VIREO 5"

Dull and nondescript—grayish above, paler below; narrow whitish eye ring and wing bar. **Habitat:** Dry scrub and pinyon-juniper thickets. **Range:** Mexican border north to s. parts of California, Nevada, Utah, Colorado, east to w. Texas (local); winters north to s. California, s. Arizona.

CASSIN'S (SOLITARY) VIREO 5"

Dull olive upperparts; greenish sides; white spectacles, wing bars, and underparts. **Habitat:** Open mixed forests; migration—parks and yards. **Range:** S. Canada to Mexican border west of Rockies; winters farther south. **Note:** Cassin's and the similar Plumbeous Vireo of the Rocky Mountains and the Blue-headed Vireo of the e. U.S. formerly were races of the Solitary Vireo.

WARBLING VIREO 5"

Olive-gray above, white below; grayish eye stripe. **Habitat:** Open deciduous woodlands; aspen, poplar groves. **Range:** S. Canada to Mexican border; winters farther south.

RED-EYED VIREO 6"

White eye stripe bordered by two black lines; gray crown; olive back, wings, and tail; whitish below; red eye at close range. **Habitat:** Woodlands, groves, shade trees. **Range:** S. parts of British Columbia east to Manitoba, but in U.S. mainly east of Rockies, south to Gulf of Mexico, local west to Washington, Montana, Colorado, Oklahoma; winters south of Mexican border.

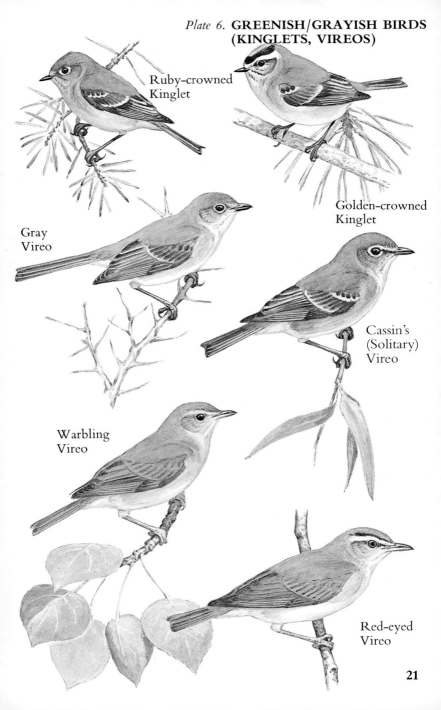

Plate 6. **GREENISH/GRAYISH BIRDS (KINGLETS, VIREOS)**

Ruby-crowned Kinglet

Golden-crowned Kinglet

Gray Vireo

Cassin's (Solitary) Vireo

Warbling Vireo

Red-eyed Vireo

Plate 7. **FLYCATCHERS**

PACIFIC-SLOPE (WESTERN) FLYCATCHER 5½"

Olive-green above, yellowish below; olivaceous wash across breast; yellowish eye ring; two whitish wing bars. **Habitat:** Moist mixed forests; parks, wooded suburbs. **Range:** S. British Columbia south along Pacific Coast and in Sierras to s. CA; winters farther south.

OLIVE-SIDED FLYCATCHER 7½"

Stout; large head; short tail; olive-green above, dark sides; yellowish white center of breast and belly; at close range—white tufts on lower back. **Habitat:** Conifer forests in clearings, burns; perches at or near tops of tall trees with dead branches, stubs. **Range:** S. British Columbia, Alberta through mountains to California-Mexico border, c. parts of AZ, NM; winters south of border.

WESTERN WOOD-PEWEE 6½"

Drab; dull olive-gray above, paler below, two wing bars. **Habitat:** Open woodlands, shade trees. **Range:** S. Canada to Mexican border; winters farther south.

SAY'S PHOEBE 7½"

Brownish gray above; blackish tail; pale grayish brown throat and breast, rusty cinnamon belly; wags tail. **Habitat:** Deserts; plains with scrub; brushy canyons; ranches; perches on fences, rocks, low buildings. **Range:** S. Canada to Mexican border, east to w. portions of Dakotas, south to TX; winters north to CA, AZ, s. NM, s. TX.

BLACK PHOEBE 7"

Black with contrasting white belly; wags or pumps tail. **Habitat:** Open woodlands; shady streams; suburbs, parks; often nests near water. **Range:** N. CA, s. NV, UT, c. AZ, NM east to w. TX south to Mexican border.

ASH-THROATED FLYCATCHER 8"

Gray-brown above; pale gray throat and breast; pale yellow belly; dusky tail with rufous webs; rufous wing edges. **Habitat:** Arid open country with scattered trees; deserts with mesquite; pinyon-juniper; open woodlands. **Range:** S. parts of WA, ID, WY south to Mexican border, east to c. TX; winters north to s. CA, AZ.

EASTERN KINGBIRD 8"

Black above, white below; broad white band at end of tail. **Habitat:** Farms, orchards; roadsides, fence posts, utility wires; lake and river shores. **Range:** S. Canada, east of Pacific Coast ranges, south to c. NV, UT, n. NM, c. TX; winters south of Mexican border.

WESTERN KINGBIRD 9"

Pale gray head, breast, and back; olive wash on back; black mask, wings, and tail; white outer tail feathers; yellow belly. **Habitat:** Open country with scattered trees; roadside fences, wires. **Range:** S. Canada to Mexican border; winters farther south.

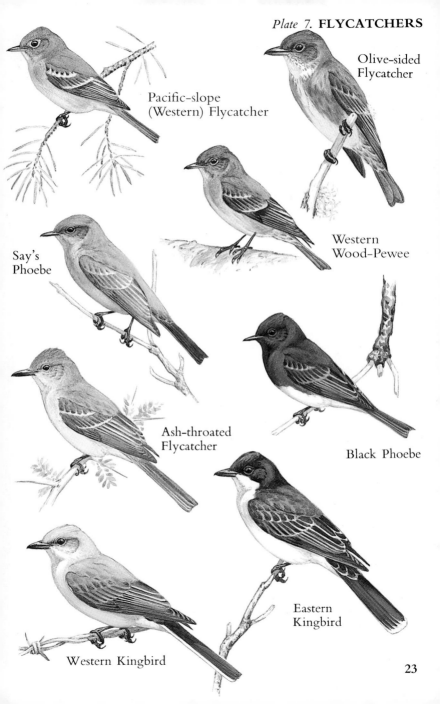

Plate 7. FLYCATCHERS

Olive-sided Flycatcher

Pacific-slope (Western) Flycatcher

Western Wood-Pewee

Say's Phoebe

Ash-throated Flycatcher

Black Phoebe

Eastern Kingbird

Western Kingbird

23

Plate 8. **LARGE GRAYISH BIRDS**

TOWNSEND'S SOLITAIRE 9"

Grayish body with dark wings and tail; whitish eye ring and outer tail feathers; buff wing patch; often perches upright. **Habitat:** Summer—mountain conifer forests; migration/winter—canyons, valleys with scrub and juniper thickets. **Range:** S. British Columbia, Alberta through mountains to Mexican border; at lower elevations in winter.

SCISSOR-TAILED FLYCATCHER 13"

Extremely long black-and-white scissor-shaped tail; pale grayish white body; bright salmon pink wing linings, flanks, belly, and vent. **Habitat:** Open country—ranches; thickets; roadsides. **Range:** TX, OK, KS north to s. NE, west to e. CO, NM, east to w. MO, AR, LA; winters south of border.

LOGGERHEAD SHRIKE 9"

Black mask, wings, and tail; gray above, white below; hooked bill. **Habitat:** Open country with scattered trees, thorn scrub; cactus deserts; roadside barbed-wire fences. **Range:** WA, s. parts of Alberta, Saskatchewan, Manitoba to Mexican border; winters north to c. states.

NORTHERN MOCKINGBIRD 10½"

Pale gray above, whitish below; long tail; large white wing tail patches, most evident in flight. **Habitat:** Mexican border; lower elevations in winter. **Range:** CA (west of Sierras) east to Dakotas, south to Mexican border.

AMERICAN DIPPER 8"

Chunky, stubtailed; slate gray; bobs up and down. **Habitat:** Mountin streams with rocks; mainly aquatic, often submerging and feeding along pebbly stream bottoms. **Range:** S. British Columbia, Alberta, w. MT, in mountains to Mexican border; lower elevations in winter.

GRAY CATBIRD 9"

Dark gray, black cap. **Habitat:** Shrubbery in parks, yards; dense thickets. **Range:** From s. Canada southeast through MT, WY, Dakotas, NE, n.e. KS; winters from s. TX south through Mexico.

CLARK'S NUTCRACKER 12½"

Chunky, short-tailed; gray head and body; black wings and tail with large white patches. **Habitat:** High mountains in conifer forests up to tree line—often seen perched on dead snags; visits campsites, feeders. **Range:** S. British Columbia, Alberta, in high mountains to c. CA, s. AZ, NM; lower elevations in winter.

GRAY JAY 11½"

Gray back, wings, and tail; paler below; whitish head with black nape (Rocky Mountains) or black hindcrown (Pacific Coast ranges). **Habitat:** Chiefly dense conifer forests; visits campsites, feeders. **Range:** S. British Columbia, Alberta, in mountains along Pacific Coast to n. CA and in Rockies to n. AZ, NM; also SD (Black Hills).

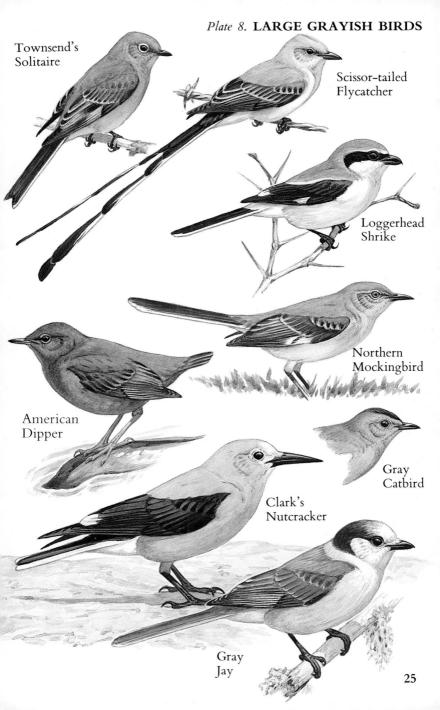

Plate 8. **LARGE GRAYISH BIRDS**

Townsend's Solitaire

Scissor-tailed Flycatcher

Loggerhead Shrike

Northern Mockingbird

American Dipper

Gray Catbird

Clark's Nutcracker

Gray Jay

25

Plate 9. **SMALL GRAYISH BIRDS**
(Gnatcatchers, Tits)

BLACK-TAILED GNATCATCHER 4½"
Black cap and tail; gray back, rump, and wings; white eye ring; whitish
below. **Habitat:** Desert scrub, arid gullies with sage, mesquite, creosote.
Range: S. CA, NV, AZ, NM, w. and s. TX.

BLUE-GRAY GNATCATCHER 4½"
Blue-gray above; white below; long black tail with white edges; white
eye ring. **Habitat:** Open mixed woods, near streams; thickets, chaparral in dry country; yards, parks. **Range:** N. CA to e. NE, south to
Mexican border; winters from CA to TX and south.

BUSHTIT 4"
Tiny, long-tailed; dull gray above, paler below; light brown cap (Pacific
Coast); same color on face (interior); some have black mask—"Black-
eared" form (Mexican border from Arizona to Texas); male—dark eye;
female—light eye. **Habitat:** Woods, pinyon-juniper, oak, chaparral.
Range: S.w. British Columbia to Mexican border; inland from WA,
ID southeast to CO, w. OK, w. TX.

VERDIN 4¼"
Gray above, whitish below; *yellow head;* chestnut shoulder patch.
Habitat: Deserts—mesquite, creosote; hummingbird feeders. **Range:**
S. CA, NV, UT, AZ, NM, w. TX to lower Gulf Coast.

OAK (PLAIN) TITMOUSE 5½"
Drab grayish brown; crest. **Habitat:** Mixed oak woodlands; parks; yards,
feeders. **Range:** S. OR through CA to Mexican border.

CHESTNUT-BACKED CHICKADEE 5"
Blackish brown cap; white cheeks; black throat; chestnut back, sides;
white below. **Habitat:** Conifers; oak, eucalyptus groves; feeders. **Range:**
Mainly Pacific Coast from s. British Columbia to c. CA.

BRIDLED TITMOUSE 4½"
Gray, black-tipped crest; black-and-white face, black throat. **Habitat:**
Oak, sycamore, pine woodlands; willows, cottonwoods, mesquite in
winter; feeders. **Range:** Mexico north to c. AZ, s.w. NM.

BLACK-CAPPED CHICKADEE 5¼"
Black cap and throat; white cheeks and below; gray back, wings, tail.
Habitat: Mixed woods, willow thickets; parks; yards; feeders. **Range:** S.
Canada to n.w. CA, from NV to Manitoba, south to KS.

MOUNTAIN CHICKADEE 5½"
Similar to previous, but white line over eye and black line through it.
Habitat: Montane conifer forests; lower elevations in winter in open
wood, groves, parks, towns; feeders. **Range:** S. Canada to California-
Mexico border, east through Rockies to extreme s.w. TX.

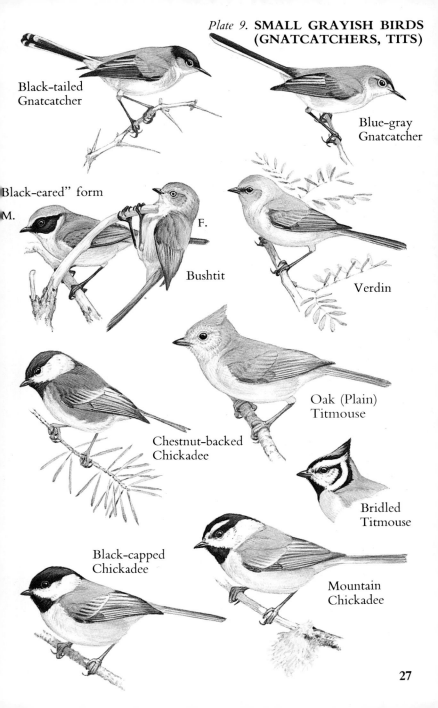

Plate 9. **SMALL GRAYISH BIRDS (GNATCATCHERS, TITS)**

Black-tailed Gnatcatcher

Blue-gray Gnatcatcher

Black-eared" form

M.

F.

Bushtit

Verdin

Oak (Plain) Titmouse

Chestnut-backed Chickadee

Bridled Titmouse

Black-capped Chickadee

Mountain Chickadee

27

Plate 10. **BLUISH BIRDS**
(Jays, Kingfisher)

PINYON JAY 10½"

All blue; *short* tail; crowlike shape. **Habitat:** Pinyon-juniper thickets, yellow pine woodlands; visits campsites, feeders. **Range:** C. Oregon, s. Montana to s.e. California, c. Arizona, New Mexico.

WESTERN SCRUB-JAY 11½"

Blue head, wings, and tail; dark cheek; brownish gray back; grayish white below with dark throat streaks. **Habitat:** Scrub oak, pinyon-juniper woodlands; chaparral; suburbs; city-park feeders. **Range:** S. parts of Washington, Idaho, Wyoming; local to Mexican border; w. Texas. **Note:** The similar-looking, but duller, Gray Jay (Plate 8) is a locally common inhabitant of montane oak canyons in s. Arizona, w. Texas (Chisos Mountains).

BLUE JAY 12"

Crested; bright blue above with white wing and tail patches; whitish below with black necklace. **Habitat:** Pine-oak woodlands; parks; yards with feeders. **Range:** Mainly east of Rockies from s. Canada to c. Texas, west to e. parts of Montana, Wyoming, Colorado.

STELLER'S JAY 13"

Crested; black head, back, and breast; deep blue wings, tail, and belly. **Habitat:** Heavy conifer forests, pine-oak woodlands; visits campsites, feeders. **Range:** S. British Columbia, Alberta, w. Montana through mountains to s. California and Mexican border, east to w. Texas.

BELTED KINGFISHER 13½"

Gray-blue and white; bushy crest; heavy spearlike bill; gray-blue breast band; female also has chestnut band lower down. **Habitat:** Lakes, ponds, rivers, streams; marshes, swamps; bays, coasts. **Range:** S. Canada to Mexican border; winters wherever there is open water.

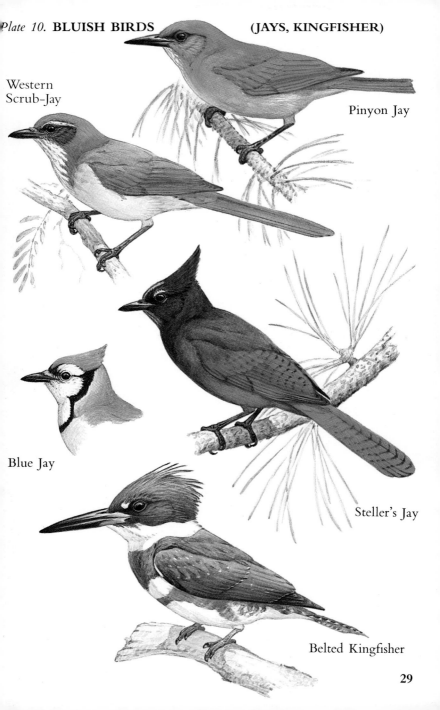

Plate 10. **BLUISH BIRDS**   (JAYS, KINGFISHER)

Western
Scrub-Jay

Pinyon Jay

Blue Jay

Steller's Jay

Belted Kingfisher

29

Plate 11. **BLUISH/REDDISH BIRDS**
(Finches, Bluebirds)

PAINTED BUNTING 5¼"
Purplish blue head; yellow-green back; bright red rump and under-parts. **Habitat:** Bushes, thickets at edges of streams, swamps; plantings along roadsides; gardens, parks; yards with feeders. **Range:** S.E. portions of Kansas, New Mexico through most of Oklahoma, Texas to Mexican border; winters farther south.

LAZULI BUNTING 5½"
Turquoise blue head and rump; reddish breast and sides; white belly and wing bar; female—gray-brown above with bluish rump; buffy below; two dull whitish wing bars. **Habitat:** Dry open woods; brushy areas near water. **Range:** S. British Columbia, Alberta, Saskatchewan to s. California, c. Arizona, New Mexico, east to Dakotas, south to w. Oklahoma, n.w. Texas; winters north to s.e. Arizona.

VARIED BUNTING 5"
Looks black at distance; close-up—mixture of deep purplish blue and brown; red nape. **Habitat:** Arid rocky slopes with thornbush, mesquite thickets. **Range:** Along Mexican border in s. portions of Arizona, New Mexico, w. and s. Texas near Rio Grande valley; winters also in last area and from Mexico southward.

INDIGO BUNTING 5½"
All blue but looks black at distance. **Habitat:** Woodland clearings, edges; brush fields, rural roadsides; lawns in migration; s.w. feeders in winter. **Range:** S. Manitoba, Dakotas to s.c. Texas, southwest to s.e. Utah, Arizona, extreme s.e. California (rare); winters south of Mexican border.

BLUE GROSBEAK 7"
Deep blue; chestnut wing patch and tawny wing bar; heavy bill. **Habitat:** Roadside thickets; swampy tangles; bushy fields. **Range:** C. California, Nevada, Utah, Colorado, Kansas north to s. North Dakota, south to Mexican border; winters north to s. Arizona.

WESTERN BLUEBIRD 7"
Deep blue above with chestnut back patch; reddish below with white belly. **Habitat:** Wooded openings; farms, orchards, roadside trees. **Range:** S. British Columbia, Alberta, w. Montana south, localized spots in higher elevations, to Mexican border, east to New Mexico, w. Texas; winters north along Pacific Coast to Washington; inland northeast to s.w. Colorado.

MOUNTAIN BLUEBIRD 7½"
Sky blue above, paler below with whitish belly. **Habitat:** Openings in conifer and mixed forests, especially in mountain meadows; winter—mainly in grasslands, deserts, agricultural areas. **Range:** s. Canada east to s.w. Manitoba, south mainly in mountains to s. California, Arizona, New Mexico, southeast to edge of Great Plains in Colorado, n.w. Oklahoma; winters from Mexico north to s.w. Washington, s. Colorado in lowlands.

Plate 11. **BLUISH/REDDISH BIRDS (FINCHES, BLUEBIRDS)**

Painted Bunting

M.

Lazuli Bunting

F.

Varied Bunting

Indigo Bunting

Blue Grosbeak

Western Bluebird

Mountain Bluebird

31

Plate 12. **GRAYISH SPARROWS**

SAGE SPARROW 5½"

Grayish above, whitish below; blackish forecrown, cheeks, and breast spot; white eye line and whisker stripe. **Habitat:** Sagebrush plains, arid scrublands; desert areas in winter. **Range:** S. Washington, Idaho, Wyoming to Mexican border; winters north to California, s. Nevada, Utah, s. New Mexico, w. Texas.

BLACK-THROATED SPARROW 5"

Black face, throat, and breast; white stripes over and under eye; white belly. **Habitat:** Cactus and creosote-bush deserts; arid, rocky slopes. **Range:** Extreme s. parts of Oregon, Idaho, s.w. Wyoming to Mexican border, east to extreme w. Colorado, southeast to w.c. Texas; winters north to s. portions of California, Arizona, New Mexico, s.w. Texas.

BLACK-CHINNED SPARROW 5¼"

Strikingly juncolike, with pink bill, dark eye, and gray head, rump, and below; otherwise sparrowlike, with streaked brown back and wings; black chin; female lacks black. **Habitat:** Arid, brushy slopes, canyons; chaparral, sagebrush. **Range:** C. California, s. Nevada, s.w. Utah east to New Mexico, extreme w. Texas, south to Mexican border; winters north to s.e. California, s. Arizona, New Mexico, s.w. Texas.

DARK-EYED JUNCO 6"

Variable; *all* forms with conspicuous pink bills, dark eyes, and white outer tail feathers. Three main types: (1) "Oregon," with black hood, brown back, and pinkish sides; (2) "Gray-headed," with pale gray head and breast, set off by bright rufous upper back; (3) "Slate-colored," with uniform slate gray color, abruptly separated by white belly. **Habitat:** Summer—conifer and mixed forests; winter-migration—nearly all possible habitats, including city parks, suburban yards with feeders. **Range:** S. Canada to Mexican border and the Gulf of Mexico.

Plate 12. **GRAYISH SPARROWS**

Black-
throated
Sparrow

Sage
Sparrow

Black-chinned
Sparrow

"Oregon"
race

"Gray-
headed"
race

"Slate-colored"
race

Dark-eyed Junco

33

Plate 13. **BROWNISH SPARROWS 1**

LARK SPARROW 6"

Head handsomely patterned in chestnut, white, and black; whitish below with dark breast spot. **Habitat:** Open country with scattered trees, bushes, hedgerows, roadside fences; prairies; orchards, farms, pastures. **Range:** S. Canada to Mexican border, east to prairie states; winter north to California, s. Arizona, New Mexico, much of Texas.

WHITE-THROATED SPARROW 6½"

White throat; yellow lores; black-and-white—or brown and buff ("tan-striped" form)—head stripes. **Habitat:** Wooded openings, clearings; lawns with shrubs in towns, city parks; feeders. **Range:** Chiefly e. North America, but winters locally in Southwest to Arizona, New Mexico, Colorado, south to Mexican border.

WHITE-CROWNED SPARROW 7"

Black-and-white head stripes; pale gray face and below; *pink* bill. **Habitat:** Thickets, hedgerows adjacent to fields; roadsides, lawns with plantings; feeders. **Range:** S. British Columbia to Mexican border, east to edge of Great Plains; winters north along Pacific Coast to British Columbia, inland to s.w. Colorado.

GOLDEN-CROWNED SPARROW 7"

Yellow crown bordered by *broad* black stripe; gray cheeks; brownish below. **Habitat:** Montane thickets, shrubs, mainly in wet areas; parks, gardens, yards; feeders. **Range:** Mainly along Pacific Coast from s. British Columbia to Mexican border.

HARRIS'S SPARROW 7½"

Black crown, face, throat, and chest; *pink* bill; grayish cheeks; white below with black spots and streaks on breast and flanks. **Habitat:** Dwarf conifer forests in high Arctic; migration/winter—open woodlands, thickets, shrubs; occasionally at feeders. **Range:** C. U.S. from e. Wyoming, South Dakota to e. Colorado, New Mexico, Texas, southeast along Mississippi River to Louisiana.

HOUSE SPARROW 6"

Large black patch on throat and chest; gray, white, and chestnut head; female—dull, dingy brown; pale eye stripe. **Habitat:** Cities, suburbs; farms; waste areas, refuse dumps. **Range:** S. Canada to Mexican border. **Note:** Introduced from Europe.

Plate 13. **BROWNISH SPARROWS 1**

Lark
Sparrow

White-throated
Sparrow

White-
crowned
Sparrow

Golden-crowned
Sparrow

Harris's
Sparrow

House Sparrow

F.

M.

Plate 14. **BROWNISH SPARROWS 2**

CHIPPING SPARROW 5¼"

Rusty cap; black-and-white eye stripes; whitish below. **Habitat:** wooded clearings, edges; farms, orchards, gardens; lawns with conifers. **Range:** S. Canada to Mexican border; winters north to s. parts of California, Arizona, New Mexico, Texas.

TREE SPARROW 6¼"

Rusty cap; grayish white below with dark breast spot; two wing bars. **Habitat:** Weedy fields, orchards, gardens, hedgerows; swampy thickets; feeders. **Range:** North of U.S.-Canada border; winters Canada to Arizona, n. California, c. Nevada, New Mexico, n. Texas.

SAVANNAH SPARROW 5½"

Heavily streaked; short, notched tail; yellowish lores; white crown stripe; pink legs. **Habitat:** Grassy fields and meadows, prairies; marsh edges; sand dunes; beaches, lake and river shores. **Range:** S. Canada to Mexican border; winters north along Pacific slope to Washington, inland to Arizona, New Mexico, Oklahoma.

RUFOUS-CROWNED SPARROW 5½"

Rufous cap; gray face and breast; black whisker line. **Habitat:** Rocky slopes with grass, scattered brush. **Range:** S.w. U.S. from c. California, s. Nevada, s.w. Utah, Arizona, s.e. Colorado, New Mexico, Oklahoma to Mexican border.

VESPER SPARROW 6"

Heavily streaked; white eye ring and outer tail feathers; close-up— chestnut shoulder. **Habitat:** Open country in dry grasslands; fields with scattered brush; sagebrush plains; farms, ranches. **Range:** S. Canada to Mexican border; winters north to s. parts of California, Arizona, New Mexico, c. Oklahoma.

SONG SPARROW 6¼"

Heavily streaked; dark breast spot; long, rounded tail, often pumped in flight. **Habitat:** Bushes and thickets along edges of moist woods, ponds, streams, swamps; roadsides; gardens, lawns and shrubs; feeders. **Range:** Canada to Mexican boarder and Gulf of Mexico; winters north to U.S.-Canada border.

FOX SPARROW 7¼"

Heavily streaked and blotched, often with dark breast spot; *reddish tail.* **Habitat:** Wooded undergrowth, dense thickets; winter—gardens, parks, yards with shrubbery; feeders. **Range:** S. British Columbia, Alberta south in mountains to s. California, c. parts of Nevada, Utah, Colorado; winters to Arizona, New Mexico, Texas, c. Oklahoma, s. Kansas. **Note:** Plumage varies geographically; darkest in Pacific Northwest.

Plate 14. **BROWNISH SPARROWS 2**

Tree
Sparrow

Chipping
Sparrow

Savannah
Sparrow

Rufous-crowned
Sparrow

Vesper Sparrow

Song
Sparrow

Fox Sparrow

Plate 15. **BROWNISH BIRDS**
(Wrentit, Wrens)

WRENTIT 6¼"
Slender with long tail, often cocked; short, thin bill; grayish brown; pale yellowish eye. **Habitat:** Chaparral; other low, dense vegetation. **Range:** Pacific Coast from n.w. Oregon to Mexican border; in California, also local inland at low elevations in n. and c. portions.

MARSH WREN 5"
Dark brown above, including solid, unmarked crown; whitish below; white eye line and back stripes. **Habitat:** Freshwater marshes with cattails, reeds, rushes; coastal salt and brackish marshes with giant reed *(Phragmites).* **Range:** S. Canada to Mexican border, but local in arid Southwest; winter north along coast to Washington, inland to s. Kansas.

HOUSE WREN 5"
Brownish above, whitish below; dark bars on wings and tail. **Habitat:** Thickets, open woodlands; orchards, gardens, parks, yards. **Range:** S. Canada to Mexican border; winters north to California, east to Texas. **Note:** Nests in cavities and bird houses.

BEWICK'S WREN 5½"
Brownish gray above, grayish white below; white eye line and tail tips; often flips tail sideways. **Habitat:** Thickets, scrub, open woods; gardens, suburban yards with shrubbery; feeders. **Range:** Pacific Coast from s.w. British Columbia to California, east from Nevada to Kansas, south to Mexican border.

CANYON WREN 5¾"
Rich reddish brown with white throat and breast. **Habitat:** Rocky canyons, cliffs—often near water; stone buildings, dams; feeders. **Range:** S. British Columbia, Washington south through Rockies to Mexican border; s.w. South Dakota southeast to w. Oklahoma, e.c. Texas.

ROCK WREN 6"
Grayish brown above with rufous rump; buff below; tawny tail tips at corners. **Habitat:** Rocky areas in arid country. **Range:** S. British Columbia, Alberta, Saskatchewan to Mexican border, east to w. Dakotas, Nebraska, Kansas, Oklahoma, Texas; winters along coast north to s. British Columbia, inland to Oklahoma.

CACTUS WREN 8"
Much larger than other wrens; chestnut crown; white eye line; streaked back; heavily barred wings and tail; conspicuous black spots below, especially on breast. **Habitat:** Deserts with cactus, mesquite, yucca, thorn scrub; also in town in arid country with similar growth; feeders. **Range:** Mexican border north to s. California, Nevada, s.w. Utah, c. Arizona, New Mexico, c. and s.w. Texas.

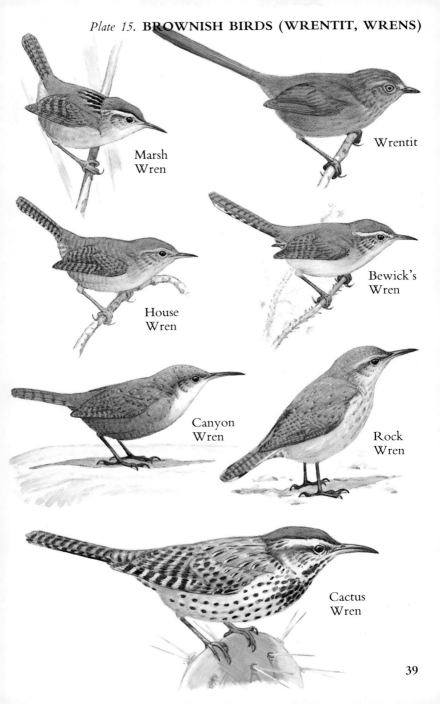

Plate 15. **BROWNISH BIRDS (WRENTIT, WRENS)**

Marsh Wren

Wrentit

House Wren

Bewick's Wren

Canyon Wren

Rock Wren

Cactus Wren

39

Plate 16. **BROWNISH BIRDS**
(Towhees, Thrashers)

GREEN-TAILED TOWHEE 7"

Rufous cap; olive-green back, wings, and tail; white throat with black whisker; gray face, breast, and sides; white belly. **Habitat:** Dry mountain slopes with scrub; winter—lower elevations with sage, chaparral, manzanita; feeders. **Range:** Oregon, Idaho, Montana to Mexican border; winters north to California, Arizona, New Mexico, Texas, to Gulf Coast.

SPOTTED (RUFOUS-SIDED) TOWHEE 8"

Black hood and upper parts; rufous sides; white belly; white back, wing, and tail spots; female—similar, but black replaced by brown. **Habitat:** Open woods; brushy fields, thickets; yards, parks; feeders. **Range:** S. Canada to Mexican border; winters on Pacific Coast, inland and north to Nevada, Utah, Colorado.

CALIFORNIA (BROWN) TOWHEE 9"

Grayish brown above, paler below; rufous vent; tawny or buffy throat with spotted necklace. **Habitat:** Brushy hills, canyons, chaparral, city; parks, gardens. **Range:** Lowlands of s. Oregon and California south through Baja Mexico.

SAGE THRASHER 8½"

Grayish above; two thin white wing bars; short bill; short tail with white-tipped corners; streaked below. **Habitat:** Sagebrush; winter— deserts. **Range:** S. Canada to California, Arizona, New Mexico; winters California, Arizona, New Mexico, w. Texas south to Mexican border.

ABERT'S TOWHEE 9"

All brown, lighter below; *black* face. **Habitat:** Desert scrub, mesquite; cottonwood-willow stands along streams in arid areas; orchards, gardens, yards; feeders. **Range:** Local in s.e. California, Nevada, s.w. Utah, w. and s. Arizona, and s.w. New Mexico to Mexican boarder.

BENDIRE'S THRASHER 10"

Grayish brown above, paler below; mottled breast. **Habitat:** Desert scrub, grasslands, ranches. **Range:** S.e. California, s. Nevada, Utah; Arizona, w. New Mexico; winters north to s. Arizona.

CURVE-BILLED THRASHER 11"

Similar to Bendire's Thrasher, with longer, more curved bill; breast more heavily mottled. **Habitat:** Deserts; canyons; towns, gardens. **Range:** Arizona, New Mexico, Colorado, Oklahoma, Texas.

CALIFORNIA THRASHER 12"

Large; very long, decurved bill; gray-brown above; line over eye; dark cheek; buffy throat, gray breast; cinnamon belly and vent. **Habitat:** Chaparral along coastal foothills; inland in brush and thickets; parks, gardens, yards. **Range:** W. and c. California south to Mexican border.

Plate 16. **BROWNISH BIRDS (TOWHEES, THRASHERS)**

Green-tailed
Towhee

Spotted
(Rufous-sided)
Towhee

California
(Brown)
Towhee

Sage
Thrasher

Abert's
Towhee

Bendire's Thrasher

Curve-billed
Thrasher

California Thrasher

41

Plate 17. **BROWNISH BIRDS**
(Waxwings, Thrushes)

CEDAR WAXWING 7"

Grayish brown; sleek and crested; black mask and chin; yellow belly and tail tip; *white* vent. **Habitat:** Orchards, fruiting trees, vines, shrubs; open woods near water. **Range:** S. Canada to Mexican border; winters north to s. British Columbia, Montana, Dakotas. **Note:** Waxwings are often very tame, and at close range the red waxlike wing spot that gives these birds their name may be seen (adults only).

BOHEMIAN WAXWING 8"

Similar to Cedar Waxwing, but larger and grayer; white spots on wings; *rusty* vent. **Habitat:** Summer—conifer forests, boreal bogs; rest of year—highly nomadic, occurring wherever there are fruiting shrubs and trees, even in towns, cities. **Range:** S. Canada south through mountains to c. California, n. Arizona, New Mexico; winters throughout.

VEERY 7"

Reddish-brown above, white below with pale gray sides; breast spots indistinct. **Habitat:** Moist deciduous woods; swampy thickets; parks, yards. **Range:** S. Canada to Utah, Colorado; farther south, migrates chiefly east of plains; winters in tropics.

SWAINSON'S THRUSH 7"

Brownish above, white below with tawny or buffy cheeks, throat, and sides; breast spots distinct; conspicuous light eye ring. **Habitat:** Moist woodlands, swampy thickets; parks, yards. **Range:** S. Canada to c. California, n. Arizona, New Mexico; winters in tropics.

HERMIT THRUSH 7"

Olive-brown above with distinct rufous tail; white below; distinct breast spots; conspicuous light eye ring. **Habitat:** Mixed woods, thickets; parks, yards. **Range:** S. Canada to Mexican border; winters along coast north to Washington, inland to Nevada, s. Utah, c. New Mexico, s. Oklahoma, nearly throughout Texas. **Note:** Often raises tail slowly.

VARIED THRUSH 9½"

Blue-gray above, orange below; orange eye stripe, wing bars, and patches; black mask and broad breast band. **Habitat:** thick, wet conifer forests; winter—also hardwoods, thickets, brushy ravines; feeders in severe winters. **Range:** Chiefly Pacific Northwest from s. British Columbia, Alberta through mountains to Idaho, n.w. Montana, n. California; winters south to California-Mexico border.

AMERICAN ROBIN 10"

Rusty breast; brownish gray back; blackish head and tail; yellow bill. **Habitat:** Lawns, golf courses, towns, parks, farms, wooded clearings. **Range:** S. Canada to Mexican border; winters throughout, except in mountains and northern Great Plains states.

Plate 17. **BROWNISH BIRDS (WAXWINGS, THRUSHES)**

Cedar
Waxwing

Bohemian
Waxwing

Veery

Swainson's Thrush

Hermit Thrush

Varied
Thrush

American
Robin

43

Plate 18. **GRASSLAND BIRDS**

CHESTNUT-COLLARED LONGSPUR 6"

Black crown, breast, and belly; chestnut nape; buff and white cheeks and throat; black crescent-shaped ear patch. **Habitat:** Tall-grass plains, prairies. **Range:** S. parts of Alberta, Saskatchewan, Manitoba through Montana, Dakotas, e. Wyoming, w. Nebraska, n. Colorado, east to w. Minnesota; winters mainly from Arizona, New Mexico, Oklahoma, Texas to Mexican border.

LAPLAND LONGSPUR 6½"

Similar to preceding, but black head and breast; also white vertical stripe on neck and in front of wing (not shown); winter—breast much duller; mostly lacks black and chestnut areas; streaky. **Habitat:** Prairies, fields, airports. **Range:** Breeds in high Arctic; winters from s. Canada to s. California, east through Great Plains, south to n. Texas. **Note:** Only the winter plumage is illustrated here; breeding dress attained in high Arctic.

SNOW BUNTING 7"

Chiefly white with black and brown patches; in flight—large white wing patches. **Habitat:** Ground bird of plains, prairies; airports, golf courses; grass flats, shores. **Range:** Breeds in high Arctic; winters from s. Canada to e. Oregon, Idaho, n. parts of Utah, Colorado, Nebraska.

AMERICAN (WATER) PIPIT 6½"

Grayish brown above; buffy breast with dark streaks; white outer tail feathers; slender bill; wags tail. **Habitat:** Ground bird of plains, prairies; freshly plowed and burned-over fields; airports, golf courses; lake and river shores, beaches, mud flats. **Range:** Breeds from s. British Columbia, Alberta, south in higher mountains to n. Arizona, New Mexico; winters from Washington to Mexican border, inland in Nevada and Great Plains states from Kansas to Texas and Gulf Coast.

HORNED LARK 7½"

Brown above, whitish below; black head and chest patches; white facial pattern; yellowish throat. **Habitat:** Ground bird of plains, prairies; short-grass fields; airports, golf courses; lake and river shores; coastal flats, beaches. **Range:** S. Canada to Mexican border.

WESTERN MEADOWLARK 9½"

Broad black V on bright yellow breast; mottled brown above; white outer tail feathers conspicuous in flight. **Habitat:** Grassy fields; airports, golf courses. **Range:** S. Canada to Mexican border; winters north along coast to s.w. British Columbia, inland to Idaho, Wyoming, Nebraska.

DICKCISSEL 6¼"

Black patch on yellow breast; chestnut wing patch; gray head; two white face stripes; female—white throat, yellow breast patch. **Habitat:** Grasslands, meadows, hayfields, especially those with alfalfa and clover; prairies; occasionally at feeders. **Range:** C. plains and prairies from Saskatchewan, Manitoba to Texas and Gulf of Mexico; winters in tropics.

Plate 18. **GRASSLAND BIRDS**

Chestnut-collared
Longspur

summer

Lapland
Longspur

winter

winter

Snow
Bunting

winter

American
(Water) Pipit

Horned
Lark

Western
Meadowlark

Dickcissel

Plate 19. **BLACKISH BIRDS 1**

PHAINOPEPLA 7½"

Glossy black; crested; broad white wing patch, conspicuous in flight; long tail; red eye at close range. **Habitat:** Arid country with mesquite, mistletoe, paloverde, other scrub; scattered oak, pepper trees. **Range:** California, s. Nevada, Utah, Arizona, New Mexico, w. Texas to Mexican border; winters in desert areas north to s. California, Arizona, s.w. New Mexico.

LARK BUNTING 7"

Black with conspicuous white wing patch; fall/winter male, female—streaked, sparrow-like, with wing patch. **Habitat:** Plains, prairies with mixture of grass, scrub, sagebrush; dry areas in winter—chiefly deserts. **Range:** S. Alberta east to s.w. Manitoba, south through Montana and Dakotas to Mexican border; winters north to s. Arizona, New Mexico, most of n. and c. Texas to extreme s. and w. Oklahoma.

BOBOLINK 7"

Mainly black; white wing patch, lower back, and rump; tawny-buff nape; fall male, female—buff below, dark brown streaks above. **Habitat:** Grassy fields, meadows; mainly marshes in fall. **Range:** S. Canada to Oregon, Colorado, Nebraska, then southeast in fall; winters in s. South America.

EUROPEAN STARLING 8"

Black at distance; chunky, short-tailed; spring/summer—iridescent green and purple; *yellow* bill: fall/winter—similar, but with white spots; *dark* bill. **Habitat:** From large cities to beaches, wooded clearings; also lawns, fields, marshes, shores, refuse dumps. **Range:** Throughout from s. Canada to Mexican border. **Note:** Introduced from Europe.

BROWN-HEADED COWBIRD 7"

Glossy black with brown head; stubby finch-like bill; female (not illustrated)—all gray. **Habitat:** Farms, fields, lawns, roadsides; wooded edges, clearings, villages, city parks; feeders. **Range:** S. Canada to Mexican border; winters north to California, Nevada, Arizona, New Mexico, Texas, Kansas. **Note:** See Bronzed Cowbird (p. 48).

YELLOW-HEADED BLACKBIRD 9½"

Black with bright golden yellow head and breast; white wing patch. **Habitat:** Freshwater marshes; ponds, streams with reedy borders; ranches; farms, fields. **Range:** S. Canada to Mexican border; winters north to c. California, s. Arizona, New Mexico, w. Texas.

RED-WINGED BLACKBIRD M. 9", F. 7"

Black with bright red shoulders, edged yellowish; female—smaller, brownish, with heavy, dark streaks; light eye stripe. **Habitat:** Marshes, meadows, hayfields; lightly wooded swamps; parks; suburban feeders. **Range:** S. Canada to Mexican border; winters north to U.S.-Canada border.

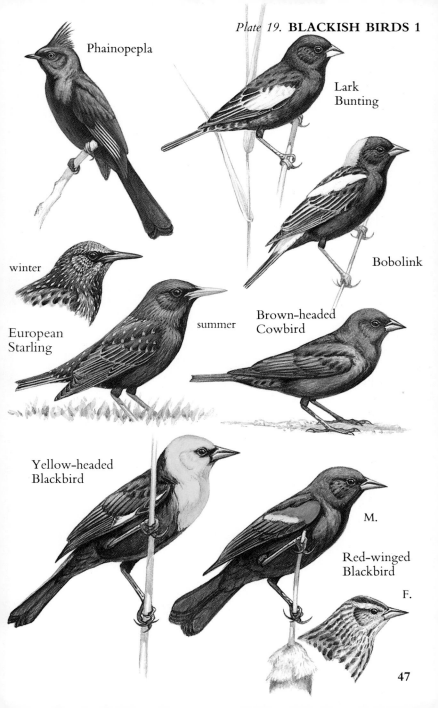

Plate 19. **BLACKISH BIRDS 1**

Phainopepla

Lark
Bunting

Bobolink

winter

European
Starling

summer

Brown-headed
Cowbird

Yellow-headed
Blackbird

M.

Red-winged
Blackbird

F.

47

Plate 20. **BLACKISH BIRDS 2**

BREWER'S BLACKBIRD 9"

Black at distance; close-up—iridescent purple head, greenish body; *yellow* eye; female—grayish, *dark* eye. **Habitat:** Open country—farms, fields, lake and river shores; city parks, suburban lawns; feeders. **Range:** S. Canada to Mexican border; winters north to s. British Columbia, ID, WY, Dakotas, s.w. NE.

BRONZED COWBIRD 8"

Black at distance; close-up—bronzy with blue-black wings and tail; *red* eye. **Habitat:** Open country with scattered trees, scrub; irrigated ranches, farmland; suburban lawns. **Range:** C. and s. AZ, s.w. NM, mainly s.c. TX to Mexican border and the Gulf of Mexico. **Note:** Unlike other birds, females of both cowbird species are parasitic, laying their eggs in other birds' nest.

COMMON GRACKLE 12"

Black at distance; close-up—iridescent blue, purple, and green; *yellow* eye; long keel- or wedge-shaped tail. **Habitat:** Farms, fields; marshes, roadsides with conifers; lawns, parks; feeders. **Range:** West to s. Alberta, MT, WY, CO, NM; winters north to s.e. NE, west to c. TX.

GREAT-TAILED GRACKLE M. 18", F. 15"

Black at distance; crow sized, slender, long, wedge-shaped tail; close-up—iridescent purple and blue; *yellow* eye; female—smaller, dark brown above, cinnamon below, darker on belly; tawny-bluff eyebrow; *yellow* eye. **Habitat:** Open areas, wetlands, ranches, towns, parks. **Range:** S.w. LA to s. CA and Mexican border, north to s. CO, NE.

AMERICAN (BLACK-BILLED) MAGPIE 20"

Generally black at distance, iridescent green and blue close-up; white belly; very long, wedge-shaped tail; two large white wing patches, very conspicuous in flight. **Habitat:** Ranches; sagebrush plains, thickets; scattered trees along water courses; at northern edge of range—also towns; feeders in severe winters. **Range:** S. Canada to s.c. CA (*not* along Pacific Coast), NM, east to edge of Great Plains as far as e. KS.

AMERICAN CROW 19"

All black; large and chunky; tail *fan shaped* in flight. **Habitat:** Farms, fields, woods, shores, parks, towns; suburban feeders. **Range:** S. Canada to California-Mexico border, c. AZ, s. NM, mainly c. and e. TX; winters north to U.S.-Canada border.

COMMON RAVEN 24"

All black; larger than American Crow; tail *wedge shaped* in flight. **Habitat:** Boreal, coniferous forests; mountains, even above tree line; rocky canyons, deserts; coastal cliffs; visits campsites, refuse dumps, where it scavenges. **Range:** S. British Columbia, Alberta south through Rockies to Mexican border; east to foothills of mountains; local in s.w. TX.

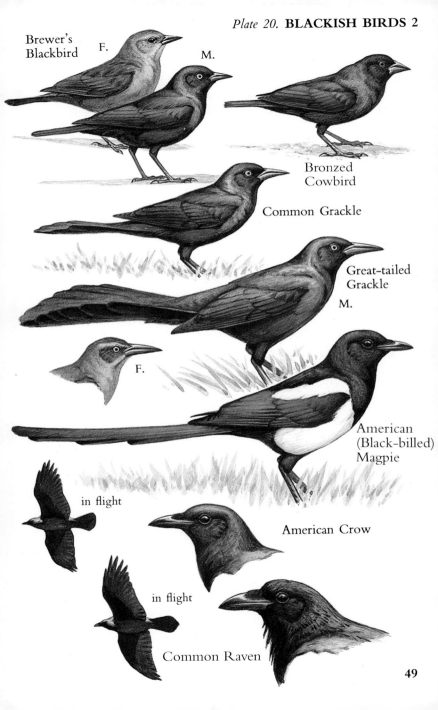

Plate 20. **BLACKISH BIRDS 2**

Brewer's
Blackbird

F.

M.

Bronzed
Cowbird

Common Grackle

Great-tailed
Grackle

M.

F.

American
(Black-billed)
Magpie

in flight

American Crow

in flight

Common Raven

49

Plate 21. **TREE CLINGERS**

PYGMY NUTHATCH 4"

Blue-gray above, buff below; grayish brown cap; whitish nape at close range. **Habitat:** Montane pine forests. **Range:** S. British Columbia, local from Washington, Idaho, Montana south through mountains to Mexican border; very local in e. Montana, Wyoming, Nevada, w. Texas.

BROWN CREEPER 5"

Brown above, white below; slender, decurved bill; stiff, pointed tail. **Habitat:** Woodlands; shade trees; shrubs, thickets. **Range:** S. Canada to Mexican border; local in Southwest.

RED-BREASTED NUTHATCH 4½"

Black-and-white striped face; blue-gray above, *rusty* below; male— *black* cap; female—*gray* cap. **Habitat:** Summer—conifer forests; winter—chiefly pines; migration—also hardwoods; feeders. **Range:** S. Canada to Mexican border; winters chiefly in lowlands.

WHITE-BREASTED NUTHATCH 5½"

Blue-gray above, *white* below; male—*black* cap; female—*gray* cap. **Habitat:** Deciduous forests; swampy woodlands; shade trees; feeders. **Range:** S. Canada to Mexican border; local in Southwest. **Note:** Nuthatches are our only birds that descend with head down.

DOWNY WOODPECKER 6½"

Black-and-white pattern; white back and below; red hindcrown; *short* bill; female—similar, but *no* red. **Habitat:** Open woodlands; orchards; shade trees; shrubbery; feeders. **Range:** S. Canada to Mexican border; local in Southwest.

LADDER-BACKED WOODPECKER 7"

White face with *black* markings; red crown *extensive.* **Habitat:** Deserts; canyons; arid scrub near water. **Range:** S.w. California, s. Nevada, s.w. Utah, Arizona, New Mexico, s.e. Colorado, w. Oklahoma to most of w. and c. Texas.

HAIRY WOODPECKER 9½"

Very similar to Downy Woodpecker, but larger and with *long* bill. Pacific Northwest form darker overall with less white in wings. **Habitat:** Forests; shade trees; feeders. **Range:** S. Canada to Mexican border; local in Southwest.

NUTTALL'S WOODPECKER 7"

Similar to Ladder-backed Woodpecker, but *black* face with *white* markings; red restricted to *hindcrown.* **Habitat:** Wooded slopes, canyons; chaparral; river groves; orchards. **Range:** Mainly w. and c. California from extreme north to Mexican border (Baja California).

Plate 21. **TREE CLINGERS**

Pygmy
Nuthatch

Brown
Creeper

Red-breasted
Nuthatch

White-breasted
Nuthatch

Downy
Woodpecker

Ladder-backed
Woodpecker

Nuttall's
Woodpecker

Hairy
Woodpecker

51

Plate 22. **WOODPECKERS 1**

RED-NAPED (YELLOW-BELLIED) SAPSUCKER 9"

Long white wing patch; red, black, and white head; yellowish belly; female—similar, but white throat. **Habitat:** Open woodlands, orchards, shade trees. **Range:** S. Canada to Mexican border, from c. Plains west to Sierras; rare to absent in Pacific states; winters mainly in southern parts of range. **Note:** The Red-naped and Red-breasted Sapsuckers formerly were geographic races of the eastern Yellow-bellied Sapsucker.

WILLIAMSON'S SAPSUCKER 9½"

Male—mostly black with long white wing patch and narrow head stripes; small red throat patch; yellow belly. Female very different—brown head; dark brown and white bars on back, wings, and sides. **Habitat:** Dry montane conifer forests. **Range:** Extreme s. British Columbia to Mexican border; east to w. Montana, c. Wyoming, Colorado, w. New Mexico; winters north to Oregon, Nevada, Utah, Arizona, New Mexico.

RED-BREASTED SAPSUCKER 9"

Long white wing patch; entirely red head and breast; yellowish belly. **Habitat:** Coniferous and mixed forests. **Range:** Chiefly Pacific slope from s. British Columbia south to Mexican border, also in Sierras; winters in most of California.

GOLDEN-FRONTED WOODPECKER 9½"

Similar to Gila Woodpecker, but male with yellow above bill and with orange nape. **Habitat:** Arid country with mesquite; dry open woodlands; pecan orchards; river groves. **Range:** S.w. Oklahoma, c. Texas to s. Gulf Coast and Mexican border.

GILA WOODPECKER 9"

Zebra backed; grayish below; male—small red cap. **Habitat:** Desert, especially with saguaro cactus; river groves in arid country; towns. **Range:** S.e. California, c. Arizona, s.w. New Mexico.

NORTHERN FLICKER 13"

Brown back with black bars; white rump; spotted below; red facial stripe on gray cheek (male only); red wing linings. **Habitat:** Open woodlands; shade trees; parks; suburban yards; often feeds on ground. **Range:** S. Canada to Mexican border; winters throughout. **Note:** May have yellow or orange wing linings in the Great Plains where they hybridize with the eastern "Yellow-shafted" form. In s.w. deserts the closely related Gilded Flicker has yellow wing linings.

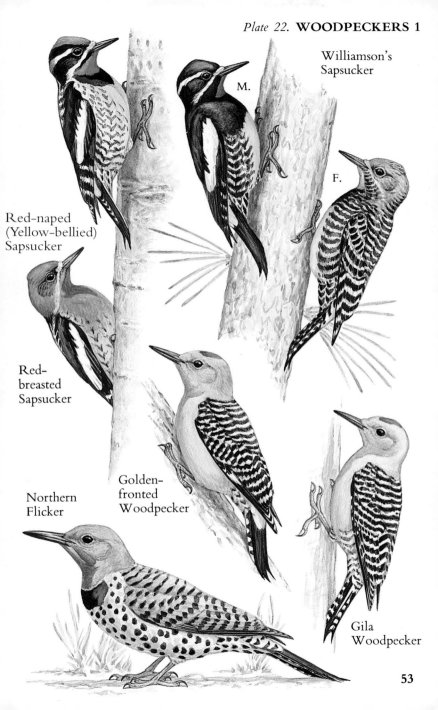

Plate 22. **WOODPECKERS 1**

Williamson's
Sapsucker

M.

F.

Red-naped
(Yellow-bellied)
Sapsucker

Red-
breasted
Sapsucker

Golden-
fronted
Woodpecker

Northern
Flicker

Gila
Woodpecker

Plate 23. **WOODPECKERS 2**

ACORN WOODPECKER 9"

Black-and-white face; red crown; black back, tail, and wings; white rump. **Habitat:** Chiefly oak-pine forests; visits campsites, hummingbird feeders. **Range:** S.w. Oregon, California to Mexican border, Arizona, New Mexico, extreme w. Texas.

LEWIS'S WOODPECKER 11"

Mainly black above, including wings, rump, and tail; gray collar and breast; rose-pink belly; dark red face. **Habitat:** Open forests in clearings, burns. **Range:** S. British Columbia, Alberta to Mexican border, east to edge of Great Plains in Wyoming, Colorado, New Mexico; winters north to Oregon, Nevada, Utah, s.w. Colorado.

RED-HEADED WOODPECKER 9½"

Red head; large white wing patches, rump, and underparts; black back, tail, and wings. **Habitat:** Groves, orchards, shade trees; farms; wooded swamps; river bottoms. **Range:** Mainly east of Rockies from s. Canada, Montana to s.c. New Mexico.

WHITE-HEADED WOODPECKER 9"

Mostly black with white forehead, cheeks, and throat; white wing patches evident in flight; male—red nape. **Habitat:** Montane conifer forests. **Range:** Washington, Oregon, w. Idaho, w. Nevada, most of California to Mexico border.

AMERICAN THREE-TOED WOODPECKER 9"

Black-and-white with bars on back and sides; male—*yellow* crown. **Habitat:** Montane conifer forests. **Range:** Local in n. plains and coniferous forest of w. Canada and Alaska; s. to n.c. Arizona in Rocky Mountain region.

PILEATED WOODPECKER 18"

Very large—crow sized; red crest; black-and-white face and neck; black body; white wing linings, conspicuous in overhead flight. **Habitat:** Mainly mixed forests, but also open woods and parks, even visiting feeders. **Range:** S. Canada, but local in west; south to c. California, in Rockies to s.c. Idaho, w. Montana; also to e. Dakotas, southeast to Kansas, Oklahoma, c. Texas.

Acorn Woodpecker

Lewis's Woodpecker

Red-headed Woodpecker

White-headed Woodpecker

American Three-toed Woodpecker

Pileated Woodpecker

Plate 23. **WOODPECKERS 2**

Plate 24. **SWALLOWS**

BARN SWALLOW 7"

Deeply forked tail; deep blue above; chestnut throat; cinnamon breast and belly. **Habitat:** Farms, fields, marshes, ponds; nests inside barns and under bridges. **Range:** S. Canada to Mexican border; winters in tropics.

CLIFF SWALLOW 6"

Square tail; buff rump; whitish forehead; chestnut to blackish throat; grayish white breast and belly. **Habitat:** Farms, marshes, lakes, rivers, cliffs; nests on cliffs and stone buildings. **Range:** S. Canada to Mexican border; winters in tropics.

BANK SWALLOW 5"

Dark brown above; white below with brown chest band. **Habitat:** Open country; feeds over land and water; nests in holes in sand and gravel banks. **Range:** Breeds locally from s. Canada to n. and c. portions of Mexican border states (*not* Arizona or Texas), but migrates through all states; winters in tropics.

VIOLET-GREEN SWALLOW 5½"

Glossy green and purple above; white on face, sides of rump, and below. **Habitat:** Canyons, cliffs; open mixed forests, clearings at high altitudes; nests in hollow trees and rock crevices; migration/winter— low elevations in fields, meadows; towns. **Range:** S. British Columbia, Alberta to Mexican border, east through Rockies to New Mexico, extreme w. Texas; winters north to Pacific Coast of c. California, locally to s. Arizona.

NORTHERN ROUGH-WINGED SWALLOW 5½"

Brown above, whitish below with dull grayish brown throat and chest. **Habitat:** Near water—nests in banks and culverts, also under bridges. **Range:** S. Canada to Mexican border; winters chiefly south of border, locally north to s. parts of California, Arizona, Texas.

AMERICAN TREE SWALLOW 6"

Glossy blue-green above, white below. **Habitat:** Open country near water; marshes, meadows; wooded swamps, especially those with dead trees; nests in holes in dead trees and next boxes. **Range:** S. Canada to s. California, Nevada, c. Arizona, New Mexico, local east of Rockies to Nebraska, Kansas; migrates through Oklahoma, Texas; winters from Mexican border north to c. California, s.w. Arizona, s. Texas.

PURPLE MARTIN 8"

Glossy purplish blue; female—similar but duller above; gray throat and breast—whitish belly. **Habitat:** Open country near water—nests around farms and towns in birdhouses, also in tree holes. **Range:** Breeds locally from s. Canada to Mexican border, but rare or absent over much of West; migrates throughout; winters in tropics.

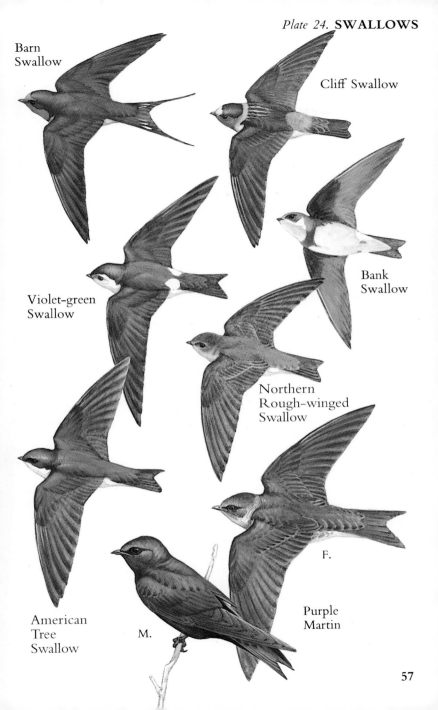

Plate 24. **SWALLOWS**

Barn
Swallow

Cliff Swallow

Bank
Swallow

Violet-green
Swallow

Northern
Rough-winged
Swallow

American
Tree
Swallow

M.

F.

Purple
Martin

Plate 25. **SWIFTS, NIGHTJARS**

VAUX'S SWIFT 4½"

Black at distance; pale whitish throat at close range; long, curved, pointed wings. **Habitat:** Open woodlands near water—nests in hollow trees; migration—open sky. **Range:** S. British Columbia, Washington, Idaho, w. Montana, local south along Pacific Coast to c. California; local migrant in s. Arizona; winters south of Mexican border.

WHITE-THROATED SWIFT 6½"

Body black-and-white from below; *notched* tail—black; long, curved, pointed wings. **Habitat:** Mountains, cliffs, canyons; nests in cliff crevices; migration—open sky. **Range:** S. British Columbia south through mountains to Mexican border, east to edge of Great Plains; winters north to c. California, s. Arizona, New Mexico, w. Texas.

BLACK SWIFT 7½"

All black; long, curved, pointed wings. **Habitat:** Mountains, cliffs—often nests behind waterfalls; migration—open sky. **Range:** Local from s. British Columbia, s.w. Alberta south through Pacific states to s. California; also n.w. Montana, c. Utah, w. Colorado; local migrant in Arizona, New Mexico; winters in tropics.

COMMON NIGHTHAWK 9½"

Long, pointed wings; in flight, prominent white wing band. **Habitat:** open country; towns, cities; open pineland; wooded clearings; farms, fields, pastures, plains. **Range:** S. Canada to Mexican border and Gulf Coast; winters in tropics.

COMMON POORWILL 7½"

Rounded wings; generally mottled grayish brown; when flushed from ground, looks like a large moth; at close range—broad white chest band. **Habitat:** Arid open country with rocks, scattered brush. **Range:** Extreme s. Canada to Mexican border; local migrant east to edge of Great Plains, winters north to s. California, Arizona, s.w. New Mexico, s.c. Texas.

Plate 25. **SWIFTS, NIGHTJARS**

Vaux's
Swift

White-throated
Swift

Black
Swift

in flight

Common Poorwill

on ground

Common
Nighthawk

59

Plate 26. **HUMMINGBIRDS**

CALLIOPE HUMMINGBIRD 3"

Our smallest bird; unique among hummers in having a "split" gorget, i.e., purplish red rays or streaks on white throat, the streaks extending to sides of neck; glittering golden green above; greenish flanks; white breast and belly. **Habitat:** Summer—high mountain forest openings, canyons, meadows; migration—lowland areas with scrub, thickets, desert. **Range:** S. Canada to CA, NV, UT, CO; migrates through Southwest to AZ, w. NM; winters south of Mexican border.

RUFOUS HUMMINGBIRD 3½"

Bright reddish brown above and on sides; fiery orange-red gorget; white chest and side of neck. **Habitat:** Forest edges, clearings; mountain meadows; lowland streams; parks, gardens. **Range:** S. Canada, n.w. CA, c. ID, w. MT; migrates east to edge of Rockies; winters chiefly in Mexico, rarely north to s. CA, AZ, TX.

ANNA'S HUMMINGBIRD 4"

Rose red cap and gorget, the latter extending slightly down sides. **Habitat:** Open woodlands; chaparral, scrub; parks, gardens. **Range:** Mainly Pacific Coast from s. British Columbia to Mexican border; also c. and s. AZ.

ALLEN'S HUMMINGBIRD 3½"

Very similar to Rufous, but crown and back iridescent green. **Habitat:** Similar to that of Rufous. **Range:** Pacific Coast from s.w. OR to s. CA; winters in n.w. Mexico, Channel Islands, rarely s. AZ.

BROAD-TAILED HUMMINGBIRD 4"

Gleaming rose red gorget. **Habitat:** Montane meadows with thickets; openings in mixed woodlands. **Range:** From e. ID, w. MT, WY to Mexican border, west to e. CA, east to w. TX; winters south of Mexican border.

COSTA'S HUMMINGBIRD 3¼"

Deep purple cap; purple gorget extending down sides. **Habitat:** Deserts, chaparral, scrub; parks, gardens. **Range:** CA, NV, AZ, NM to Mexican border; winters north to s. CA, AZ.

BLACK-CHINNED HUMMINGBIRD 3½"

Gorget with black chin and bluish purple throat, snow white chest; greenish sides; at distance—gorget looks black; female—greenish above, whitish below. **Habitat:** Deserts, scrub, chaparral, canyons, river groves; parks, gardens. **Range:** S. Canada to Mexican border, east to ID, MT, WY, CO, TX; winters south of Mexican border.

BROAD-BILLED HUMMINGBIRD 3¼"

Black in distance; close-up—all dark green with white vent; *red* bill with black tip; in good light—dark *blue* gorget. **Habitat:** Desert canyons; slopes with agaves, cacti, mesquite, ocotillo; woodland openings. **Range:** S.e. AZ, s.w. NM, w. TX; winters in Mexico.

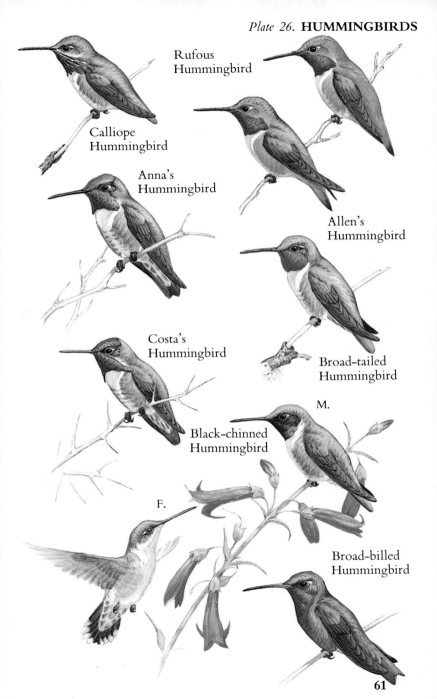

Plate 26. **HUMMINGBIRDS**

Rufous
Hummingbird

Calliope
Hummingbird

Anna's
Hummingbird

Allen's
Hummingbird

Costa's
Hummingbird

Broad-tailed
Hummingbird

M.

Black-chinned
Hummingbird

F.

Broad-billed
Hummingbird

Plate 27. **CUCKOO, PIGEONS**

YELLOW-BILLED CUCKOO 12"

Brown above, white below; slender; long-tailed; bill slightly down-curved, lower half yellow; large white patches on underside of tail; rufous flash in wings, evident in flight. **Habitat:** Open woodlands; thickets; overgrown fields; orchards. **Range:** SD, s. WY, UT, c. NV, s. CA to Mexican border; winters in tropics.

COMMON GROUND-DOVE 6½"

Very small; pinkish gray; *short, rounded,* dark tail; rufous outer wing patch, conspicuous in flight; at close range—scaly head and breast. **Habitat:** Open sandy areas with scattered trees, scrub; orchards, gardens; ranches; towns; feeders. **Range:** S. CA, AZ, NM, TX.

MOURNING DOVE 12"

Slender; fawn colored; long, pointed tail, edged white. **Habitat:** Open country; lawns, parks; feeders. **Range:** S. Canada to Mexican border; winters nearly throughout, except Canada and northern border states.

INCA DOVE 8"

Similar to Common Ground-Dove, but with *long, pointed,* white-edged tail. **Habitat:** Arid areas with cactus, mesquite; gardens, parks, yards; feeders. **Range:** S.e. CA, s. AZ, NM, much of c. and s. TX.

WHITE-WINGED DOVE 12"

Generally gray; large white wing patches, most conspicuous in flight; rounded tail, corners tipped white. **Habitat:** Arid country with mesquite, paloverde, saguaro; riverine woodlands, orchards; feeders. **Range:** S.e. CA, s. AZ, s.w. NM, southeast along Mexican border to southernmost TX on the Rio Grande River.

SPOTTED DOVE 13"

Easily identified by black collar with white spots; long, rounded tail with white edge. **Habitat:** Suburban gardens, yard, city parks; farms; wooded edges. **Range:** S. CA. **Note:** Introduced from China.

BAND-TAILED PIGEON 15"

Large and plump; gray; fan-shaped tail with dark band across middle; purplish head and breast; at close range—narrow white crescent on nape; yellow bill with black tip. **Habitat:** Montane oak, pine forests; winter—also parks, suburban gardens; feeders. **Range:** Mountains along Pacific Coast from s. British Columbia to Mexican border; inland mountains from NV, UT, CO to s. AZ, NM, w. TX; winters chiefly south of Mexican border, locally in CA.

ROCK (DOVE) PIGEON 13"

Plump; blue-gray body; short, fan-shaped tail; white rump; two black wing bars; iridescent neck patch. **Habitat:** Rock cliffs—its ancestral home; cities, towns; parks, farms; dumps. **Range:** Throughout, from Canada to Mexican border. **Note:** Introduced from Europe. Many color varieties occur, ranging from black to white.

Plate 27. **CUCKOO, PIGEONS**

Yellow-billed
Cuckoo

Common
Ground-Dove

Mourning
Dove

Inca Dove

White-winged
Dove

Spotted
Dove

Band-tailed
Pigeon

Rock
(Dove)
Pigeon

Plate 28. **SMALL GAME BIRDS**

NORTHERN BOBWHITE 9½"

Small chickenlike bird; black-and-white face; female—similar, but with tawny-buff face. **Habitat:** Farmland; hedgerows, roadsides; fields with thickets, dense brush; feeders. **Range:** West to e. portions of Wyoming, Colorado, New Mexico, south through most of Texas.

SCALED QUAIL 11"

Grayish brown with white-tipped crest; scaled pattern over much of body. **Habitat:** Arid areas with thorn scrub; dry grasslands. **Range:** Local from s.e. Colorado, s.w. Kansas through w. Oklahoma, Texas, New Mexico, s.e. Arizona.

MOUNTAIN QUAIL 11"

Brown above; gray crown and breast; *chestnut* throat and sides; black-and-white streaks on neck and blanks; conspicuous long, *upright* head plume(s). **Habitat:** Mountain slopes, both forested and open, but almost always with undergrowth. **Range:** Local from Canadian border south through Washington, w. Idaho, Oregon, Utah, w. Nevada, California to Mexican border.

GAMBEL'S QUAIL 11"

Variegated—brown, gray, buff, and chestnut; *black* throat and *belly patch;* conspicuous black head plume—curved forward. **Habitat:** Desert scrub; thickets; common at *feeders.* **Range:** Mexican border north to s.e. California, s. Nevada, Arizona, New Mexico, w. Texas; local north to Utah, Colorado.

CALIFORNIA QUAIL 11"

Similar to Gambel's Quail, but with *chestnut belly patch* and more scaling. **Habitat:** *Woodland* edges; clearings; coastal scrub (chaparral); farms; parks; suburban yards—often near water. **Range:** Chiefly Pacific slope from s. British Columbia to Mexican border; inland east to Idaho, Nevada, Utah, where apparently introduced. **Note:** The habitat differences in these species help to distinguish them.

CHUKAR 13"

Grayish brown body with buff belly and vent; *red* bill and legs; prominent *black line* outlining white throat; black side stripes. **Habitat:** Arid, rocky slopes; canyons. **Range:** Local throughout much of West in mountainous areas. **Note:** Introduced from Eurasia.

GRAY PARTRIDGE 13"

Prominent *rusty face* and *throat;* chestnut side stripes and belly patch; otherwise brown above, gray below. **Habitat:** Open agricultural districts; grassy plains, prairies. **Range:** Local; s. Canada, n. U.S. to c. states. **Note:** Introduced from Eurasia.

Plate 28. **SMALL GAME BIRDS**

Northern
Bobwhite

Scaled
Quail

Mountain
Quail

Gambel's
Quail

Chukar

California
Quail

Gray
Partridge

65

Plate 29. **ROADRUNNER, LARGE GAME BIRDS**

GREATER ROADRUNNER 22"

Large *long-tailed* ground cuckoo with *bushy crest;* heavily streaked. **Habitat:** Stony deserts with scrub, mesquite; sometimes bold and unwary, frequenting feeders, patios, even house rooftops. **Range:** S.w. U.S. from c. California east to extreme w. parts of Arkansas, Louisiana; also s.w. Missouri. **Note:** Most numerous in s.w. deserts.

WILD TURKEY M. 48", F. 36"

Huge gallinaceous bird; bare head and neck with blue and red wattles; male—bristly "beard" on breast; female—smaller and duller without much ornamentation. **Habitat:** Hardwood forests, mainly at higher elevations. **Range:** Chiefly Rocky Mountains, but local over much of West. **Note:** Wild Turkeys have chestnut tail tips; domesticated varieties white ones.

RING-NECKED PHEASANT M. 33", F. 23"

Very long, pointed tail; white neck ring; iridescent purple and green head; scarlet face wattles; female—smaller and much duller; mottled brown above, tawny-buff below. **Habitat:** Farmland with hedgerows, cornfields; thickets near marshes, swamps; feeders. **Range:** Nearly throughout, but local over much of Southwest. **Note:** Introduced from s. Asia.

SHARP-TAILED GROUSE 17"

Brownish; covered with *speckles and spots.* **Habitat:** Grasslands; savannas; sagebrush; wooded edges. **Range:** Local from s. Canada to c. U.S.; *not* along Pacific slope.

GREATER SAGE-GROUSE 28"

Large; brownish gray above; black throat, neck, and belly; white breast; long, pointed, spiked tail; at close range—male has yellow eye wattles. **Habitat:** Open sagebrush plains. **Range:** S. Alberta, Saskatchewan south through the plains, foothills of Rocky Mountain states, west to e. Washington, Oregon, California, south to n.e. New Mexico.

BLUE GROUSE 18"

Deep gray body; whitish rump; black tail; pale gray band at tail tip; orange head wattle or "comb" above eye. **Habitat:** Conifer forests, mainly at high altitudes. **Range:** S. British Columbia, Alberta, in mountains south to c. California, n. Arizona, s.w. New Mexico.

RUFFED GROUSE 17"

Variously brown to gray above, paler below; black neck patch; broad black band near tail tip; slight crest. **Habitat:** Open mixed woodlands; forest clearings. **Range:** S. Canada to n. California, Utah, extreme s.w. South Dakota (Black Hills).

Plate 29. **ROADRUNNER, LARGE GAME BIRDS**

Greater Roadrunner

Wild Turkey

Ring-necked
Pheasant
M.

F.

Sharp-tailed
Grouse

Greater
Sage-Grouse

Blue
Grouse

Ruffed
Grouse

Plate 30. **HAWKS 1**
(Vultures, Eagles)

BLACK VULTURE 25"

Black; white patches near wing tips evident in flight; short tail; distinctive flight—several flaps and a glide; at close range—small gray head. **Habitat:** Open country; towns; limited mainly to lower elevations. **Range:** S. and c. Texas, extreme s. Arizona.

TURKEY VULTURE 28"

In flight, wings held in shallow V, tilting from side to side; undersurface of wings two-toned; at close range—small red head; immature—gray head. **Habitat:** Generally open country—wherever carrion is found, both in mountains and lowlands. **Range:** S. Canada to Mexican border; winters north to California, Arizona, New Mexico, s. Kansas.

GOLDEN EAGLE 33"

Dark brown overall; at close range—golden wash on head and neck. **Habitat:** Mountains, plains, canyons, deserts. **Range:** S. Canada to Mexican border, rare in c. and s. Texas. **Note:** Immatures have conspicuous white base of tail with broad, black terminal band; white patches in wings.

BALD EAGLE 33"

Dark brown body and wings; white head and tail; large yellow bill. **Habitat:** Lakes, rivers, seacoasts. **Range:** S. Canada to Mexican border and Gulf of Mexico; local in much of the interior away from water. **Note:** Immatures have dark heads and tails; variable white mottling in wing linings and base of tail; large dark beak. Mature to adult plumage in four years.

Plate 30. **HAWKS 1 (VULTURES, EAGLES)**

Black
Vulture

Turkey
Vulture

Golden
Eagle

Bald
Eagle

Plate 31. **HAWKS 2**
(Buteos)

RED-TAILED HAWK 23"

Reddish tail; white or buff breast; dark streaks on belly. **Habitat:** Chiefly open country near woodlands—plains, prairies, deserts. **Range:** S. Canada to Mexican border; winter—withdraws from Canada, Montana, Dakotas. **Note:** This species is extremely variable, ranging from dark to very pale in color, but most adults may be identified by reddish tails.

RED-SHOULDERED HAWK 21"

Chestnut shoulders, body (below), and wing linings; tail with broad black bands and narrow white ones. **Habitat:** Wooded swamps, moist forests near rivers. **Range:** E. Nebraska, c. Kansas, w.c. parts of Oklahoma, Texas to Mexican border and Gulf Coast; Pacific slope of California.

SWAINSON'S HAWK 21"

Pale throat; dark breast; light-colored belly (white to reddish); light wing linings, dark flight feathers; in flight, tilts somewhat-pointed wings upward like a harrier; banded tail with broader band near tip. **Habitat:** Open country with scattered trees—plains, prairies, deserts. **Range:** Local from s. Canada to Mexican border; winters chiefly in s. South America. **Note:** Dark, almost blackish forms also occur.

ROUGH-LEGGED HAWK 23"

Light phase—broad dark band near tip of white tail; dark patch at bend of mostly white in wing; dark belly; dark phase—mainly black, but with much white in wing and tail from below. **Habitat:** Fields, prairies, plains, marshes, coastal areas. **Range:** Winters from s. Canada to Mexican border, but rare in s. parts from California east to Texas.

FERRUGINOUS HAWK 14"

Rufous back and shoulders; whitish or pale head and tail; tail suffused with rusty color; in flight from below—mainly white; chestnut legs, when folded, form a conspicuous V, evident when bird is overhead. **Habitat:** Dry open country, chiefly Great Plains, but also ranches and desert areas in winter. **Range:** Washington, s. parts of Alberta, Saskatchewan, North Dakota to w. portions of Nebraska, Kansas, Oklahoma, Texas, south to Mexican border; winters north to s.c. Oregon, c. Nevada, n.e. Utah, s.e. Wyoming, s.w. South Dakota.

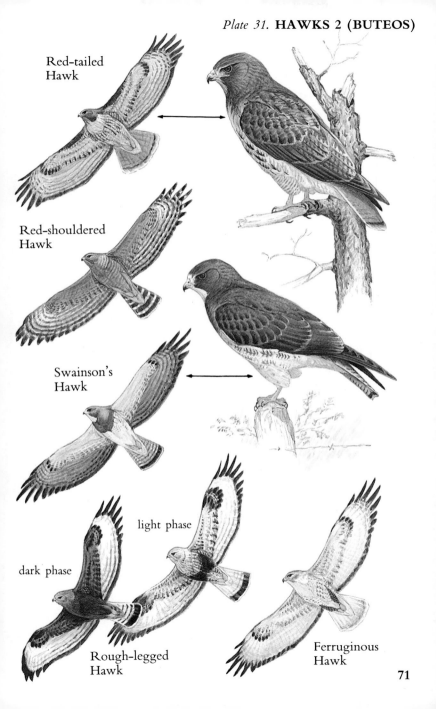

Plate 31. **HAWKS 2 (BUTEOS)**

Red-tailed
Hawk

Red-shouldered
Hawk

Swainson's
Hawk

light phase

dark phase

Rough-legged
Hawk

Ferruginous
Hawk

71

Plate 32. **HAWKS 3**
(Accipiters, Osprey, Harrier)

SHARP-SHINNED HAWK 12"

Small woodland hawk; short, rounded wings; long tail; blue-gray above, finely barred rusty red below. Immature—brown above, streaked below. Flies with several flaps and a glide. **Habitat:** Woodlands. **Range:** S. Canada to Mexican border; winters north to Washington, s. Idaho, Wyoming, s.e. Nebraska.

OSPREY 24"

Large, long-winged; dark above, white below; black patch at bend of wings; dark facial patch. Flies with downward bend or crook in wing. **Habitat:** Seacoast, lake, river. **Range:** Local from s. Canada to Mexican border; rare to absent in dry open country; winters in n. to s. California, s. Texas.

NORTHERN GOSHAWK 23"

Large woodland hawk; broad, rounded wings; blue-gray above, pearl-gray below; white line over eye. Immature—brown above, streaked below, with pale line over eye. **Habitat:** Heavy coniferous and mixed forests; montane forests in s. portions of range; more open areas in winter. **Range:** S. Canada to mountains of n. Mexico; rare to absent east of Rockies, s. California, most of Texas.

NORTHERN HARRIER (MARSH HAWK) M. 19", F. 22"

White rump; long wings and tail; male—pearl-gray above, pale below; female—larger brown above, streaked below; immature—rusty below, no streaks. **Habitat:** Marsh, field, prairie, ranches, shoreline, beach. **Range:** S. Canada to Mexican border; winters locally north to coast of s. British Columbia, inland to s. parts of Wyoming, Nebraska.

Plate 32. **HAWKS 3 (ACCIPITERS, OSPREY, HARRIER)**

Osprey

Sharp-shinned
Hawk

ad.

imm.

Northern
Goshawk

Northern
Harrier (Marsh Hawk)

F.

M.

73

Plate 33. **HAWKS 4**
(Kites, Falcons)

WHITE-TAILED (BLACK-SHOULDERED) KITE 16"

Falcon shaped with long *white* tail; long, pointed wings with dark flight feathers (below) and *black* shoulders (above); white underparts, including head and wing linings; pearl-gray back. **Habitat:** Savannas, grasslands; ranches; marshes; along rivers and estuaries. **Range:** W. Oregon, most of California to Mexican border; southernmost Texas. **Note:** Often hovers over one spot—like a kestrel.

MISSISSIPPI KITE 14"

Falcon shaped with long *black* tail; long, pointed wings with black flight feathers; whitish rectangular patch at rear end of wings; head whitish; dark gray back and shoulders; pearl-gray below. **Habitat:** Open woodlands near water; prairies, plains with scattered trees (savannas). **Range:** Texas, Oklahoma, Kansas west to s.e. Colorado, New Mexico, e.c. Arizona, south to Mexican border; winters in tropics.

AMERICAN KESTREL (SPARROW HAWK) 11"

Long, pointed wings; reddish back and tail; blue-gray wings; black-and-white facial pattern; black band near tail tip; female—similar, but tail barred and wings reddish like back. **Habitat:** Open country— farms, fields, beaches, shores; cities. **Range:** S. Canada to Mexican border; winters along coast north to British Columbia, inland north to c. Idaho, s.w. Montana, s. Wyoming, n.e. Colorado, s. Nebraska.

MERLIN (PIGEON HAWK) 12"

Long, pointed wings; heavily streaked below; banded tail; male—blue-gray above; female and immature—dark brown above. **Habitat:** Open country—beaches, fields, marshes, thickets, light woods. **Range:** S. Canada, northern tier of states south in mountains to Oregon, s. Idaho, Wyoming, Dakotas; winters along coast north to s. British Columbia, but inland only as far as the s. parts of Nevada, Arizona, New Mexico, Texas.

PEREGRINE FALCON 18"

Slate black above, buff below with dark bars; contrasting black-and-white face. **Habitat:** Open country with cliffs, especially near water; more rarely in cities with tall buildings; also bridges. **Range:** Local throughout, from s. Canada to Mexican border.

PRAIRIE FALCON 18"

Light brown above, paler below with dark streaks and spots; narrow vertical patches on white face. Best field mark is *black* base and center of wing linings when bird is in overhead flight. **Habitat:** Dry open country with cliffs, canyons; buttes, mesas in deserts and plains. **Range:** S. Canada to Mexican border; winters north to s. portions of Washington, Idaho, Montana, Dakotas.

Plate 33. **HAWKS 4 (KITES, FALCONS)**

White-tailed
(Black-shouldered) Kite

Mississippi
Kite

American
Kestrel
(Sparrow Hawk)

M.

Merlin

F.

Peregrine
Falcon

Prairie
Falcon

Plate 34. **SMALL OWLS**

ELF OWL 5½"

Sparrow sized—smallest owl in the world; very short tail; brownish overall with indistinct rusty markings on white underparts. **Habitat:** Saguaro deserts; oak and sycamore canyons. **Range:** Mainly c. and s. Arizona; s.w. New Mexico; local in w. and s. Texas; winters in Mexico.

NORTHERN PYGMY-OWL 7"

Long dark brown tail with narrow whitish bars; white-spotted crown and wings; black patches on each side of nape; white below with dark streaks; two color phases—brown and gray. **Habitat:** Open mixed montane forests, wooded canyons. **Range:** S. British Columbia, Alberta through Rockies to Mexican border; ranges southeast to e. parts of Colorado, New Mexico.

NORTHERN SAW-WHET OWL 8"

Short tail; streaked forehead; white below with reddish brown streaks. **Habitat:** Thick coniferous and mixed forests; winter—evergreen groves, thickets. **Range:** S. Canada to Mexican border, but farther east only to c. Texas. **Note:** Very tame—can sometimes be taken alive by hand!

WESTERN SCREECH-OWL 9"

Head tufts widely spaced; heavily mottled and streaked below; two color phases—gray and russet brown (mostly in Pacific Northwest). **Habitat:** Open woods, farm groves, orchards, suburbs, city parks. **Range:** S. British Columbia, Washington, Idaho, w. Montana south to Mexican border, east to w. Texas.

BURROWING OWL 9"

Long legs; spotted forehead; white chin; barred below. **Habitat:** *Ground* owl of open country—grasslands, prairies, plains, deserts; also airports; often perches on fences, roadside wires. **Range:** Local from s. Canada to Mexican border and Gulf Coast; winters north to c. California, s. Arizona, s.e. New Mexico, w.c. Texas.

Plate 34. **SMALL OWLS**

Elf Owl

Northern Pygmy-Owl

Northern Saw-whet Owl

Western Screech-Owl

Burrowing Owl

Plate 35. **LARGE OWLS**

BARN OWL 17"

White heart-shaped face; *dark* eyes; pale buff to cinnamon below with dots; rusty brown above; long legs. **Habitat:** Chiefly open country—cliffs; large hollow trees; old buildings, silos, water towers, lighthouses; city parks. **Range:** U.S.-Canada border to Mexican border and Gulf Coast; winters north to Washington, s. Idaho, Wyoming, s. South Dakota.

SPOTTED OWL 18"

Dark eyes; dark brown above and below, with creamy white spots and blotches. **Habitat:** Thick forests—mainly conifers; also hardwoods in canyons. **Range:** Local over much of range—(1) Pacific slope from s.w. British Columbia to s. California; (2) s. Rocky Mountains from s. Utah, c. Colorado through Arizona, New Mexico, extreme w. Texas to c. Mexico.

SHORT-EARED OWL 15½"

Tawny-buff; heavily streaked below. **Habitat:** Fields, prairies, plains, marshes, beaches; also airports, refuse dumps. **Range:** S. Canada to Mexican border; winters north to U.S.-Canada border.

GREAT HORNED OWL 22"

Head tufts widely spaced; white throat; finely barred below. **Habitat:** Extremely adaptable—from heavy forests, woodlots, swamps, and river bottoms to rocky deserts, cliffs, and canyons; even in large trees in city parks. **Range:** Widely distributed—from s. Canada to Mexican border and Gulf of Mexico.

LONG-EARED OWL 15"

Head tufts close together; streaked and mottled below. **Habitat:** Forests, thickets; winter—conifer groves. **Range:** S. Canada to Mexican border; but farther east only to c. Texas.

Plate 35. **LARGE OWLS**

Barn Owl

Spotted
Owl

Short-eared
Owl

Great Horned
Owl

Long-eared
Owl

Plate 36. **GEESE, SWANS**

CANADA GOOSE 35"

Largest goose; long black neck and head; white chinstrap; light brown body. **Habitat:** Lakes, rivers, bays, inlets, marshes; grassy and cultivated (grain) fields. **Range:** S. Canada to Mexican border; winters along coast north to s. British Columbia, inland to s. parts of Oregon, Idaho, Wyoming, South Dakota.

BRANT 25"

Small, Mallard sized; short black neck and head; whitish below. **Habitat:** Bays, estuaries, salt marshes, tidal flats—essentially a marine goose. **Range:** Pacific Coast from British Columbia to Mexican border.

GREATER WHITE-FRONTED GOOSE 30"

Medium sized; grayish brown with irregular black bars and blotches below; bill and legs pink to orange; at close range—white frontal band at base of bill, giving bird its name. **Habitat:** Mainly freshwater areas—lakes, marshes, flooded fields, grasslands. **Range:** Local from s. Canada to Mexican border; winters chiefly in Pacific states, also in small portions of Idaho, Montana, Wyoming, Utah, e. New Mexico, s. Texas; migrates nearly throughout.

SNOW GOOSE 30"

Medium sized; white phase—white with much black in wings; immature—pale gray; "blue" phase—dark grayish brown with white head and upper neck. **Habitat:** Marshes, ponds, bays; cutover grain fields. **Range:** S. Canada to Mexican border; winters chiefly in California, also locally in s. Arizona, e. New Mexico, s. Texas; migrates nearly throughout.

TRUMPETER SWAN 65"

Our largest waterfowl; similar to Tundra (Whistling) Swan but much larger; also heavier bill. **Habitat:** Chiefly inland lakes and marshes. **Range:** Sedentary—restricted in Canada to s. British Columbia, Alberta, s.w. Saskatchewan; in n.w. U.S. to Washington, s.e. Oregon, w. Montana, e. Idaho, n.w. Wyoming, South Dakota.

TUNDRA (WHISTLING) SWAN 53"

All white; very long neck; black bill. **Habitat:** Lakes, rivers, bays, flooded fields. **Range:** Local from s. Canada to Mexican border; winters on Pacific Coast north to s. British Columbia, inland to s. Idaho, w. Utah, locally in s. Arizona, New Mexico, w. Texas.

Plate 36. **GEESE, SWANS**

Canada
Goose

Brant

White-fronted
Goose

blue phase
Snow Goose

in flight

Snow Goose
white phase

Trumpeter
Swan

Tundra
(Whistling)
Swan

81

Plate 37. **TIPPING DUCKS 1**

MALLARD 24"

Bright green head; yellow bill; white neck ring; chestnut breast; blue wing patch bordered with white bars; female—mottled brown; orange bill with brown patch. **Habitat:** Marshes, ponds, lakes, rivers, bays, flooded fields. **Range:** S. Canada to Mexican border.

GADWALL 21"

Dark gray; brown head and neck; small white wing patch, evident in flight. **Habitat:** Marshes, ponds, rivers. **Range:** S. Canada to Mexican border; winters along Pacific Coast north to s. British Columbia, inland to Idaho, s.e. Colorado, Kansas.

AMERICAN WIGEON (BALDPATE) 20"

White crown; green head patch; *large* white wing patch, evident in flight. **Habitat:** Ponds, lakes, rivers, marshes, lagoons, bays, estuaries. **Range:** S. Canada to Mexican border; winters along Pacific Coast north to s. British Columbia, inland to s. Nevada, Arizona, s. New Mexico, w. and s. Texas.

NORTHERN PINTAIL 27"

White vertical line on side of dark brown head; white neck and breast; gray body; long, pointed tail. **Habitat:** Marshes, ponds, rivers. **Range:** S. Canada to Mexican border; winters north to s. British Columbia, w.c. Washington, s.w. Idaho, w. Utah, c. Colorado, s.e. Nebraska.

FULVOUS WHISTLING-DUCK 19"

Tawny body; all-black wings, evident in flight. **Habitat:** Shallow water in marshes, lagoons, rice fields, estuaries. **Range:** Mexican border north to c. California, s.w. Arizona; also s. Texas along Gulf of Mexico.

BLACK-BELLIED WHISTLING-DUCK 21"

Gray face and bright *reddish* bill; chestnut neck, breast, and back; black belly; pink legs; large white wing patch. **Habitat:** Wooded ponds, streams; marshes, lagoons. **Range:** S. portions of Arizona, Texas.

Plate 37. **TIPPING DUCKS 1**

M.

Mallard

F.

Gadwall

American Wigeon (Baldpate)

Northern
Pintail

Fulvous
Whistling-Duck

Black-bellied
Whistling-Duck

Plate 38. **TIPPING DUCKS 2**

GREEN-WINGED TEAL 14"

Chestnut head with green patch; white vertical line in front of wing; gray body; green wing patch, evident in flight. **Habitat:** Marshes, ponds, estuaries. **Range:** S. Canada to Mexican border; winters north to coastal Washington, inland to c. Idaho, s.w. Montana, Wyoming, s.w. Nebraska.

BLUE-WINGED TEAL 16"

White crescent behind bill; light blue wing patch, evident in flight. **Habitat:** Marshes, ponds, lagoons. **Range:** S. Canada to Mexican border; winters north only to c. California, s. Texas, otherwise south of Mexican border.

CINNAMON TEAL 17"

Cinnamon red head and body; light blue wing patch, evident in flight. **Habitat:** Marshes, ponds, lagoons. **Range:** S. parts of British Columbia, Alberta, Saskatchewan to Mexican border, east to w. edge of Great Plains; winters north to c. California, s. parts of Arizona, New Mexico, Texas.

NORTHERN SHOVELER 20"

Long, shovel-shaped bill, held pointed downward; green head; white chest; chestnut sides; light blue wing patch, evident in flight. **Habitat:** Marshes, ponds, lagoons, estuaries. **Range:** SS. Canada to Mexican border; winters north to Oregon, Nevada, Utah, c. New Mexico, Oklahoma.

WOOD DUCK 18½"

Gaudily colored in green, purple, blue, and white; chestnut breast; at close range—red eye and base of bill; swept-back crest; female—dull, mostly grayish; prominent white eye patch. **Habitat:** Swamps, marshes, wooded ponds, streams. **Range:** Local along Pacific Coast from s. British Columbia to Mexican border; inland from s. Manitoba, Washington, Oregon, c. Idaho, s.w. Montana, n. Wyoming, Dakotas to Arizona, c. Colorado, n.w. and s. New Mexico, Kansas, Oklahoma, nearly all of Texas; winters north to Washington, Arizona, New Mexico, c. Colorado, s.e. Kansas.

Plate 38. **TIPPING DUCKS 2**

Green-winged Teal

Blue-winged
Teal

Cinnamon Teal

Northern
Shoveler

F.

Wood Duck

M.

85

Plate 39. **DIVING DUCKS 1**

GREATER SCAUP 18"

Black fore and aft; light in the middle; close-up—head rounded with green gloss, bill broad with large "nail" on tip; female—brownish with distinct white patch at base of bill. **Habitat:** Lakes, rivers, bays, estuaries, Pacific coastal waters, and Gulf of Mexico. **Range:** Winter—s. British Columbia to Mexican border; restricted mainly along Pacific Coast; rare and local inland.

LESSER SCAUP 16½"

Both sexes nearly identical to Greater Scaup, but smaller with more delicate bill, slightly crested profile; male's head with purplish gloss. **Habitat:** Marshes, lakes, rivers, bays. **Range:** S. Canada to Mexican border; winters locally north along Pacific Coast to s. British Columbia, inland to Great Basin area.

RING-NECKED DUCK 16½"

Black head, back, and breast; white wedge in front of wing; pale gray sides; pale blue bill with white ring and black tip; at close range—purplish gloss on head. **Habitat:** Wooded ponds, lakes, rivers. **Range:** Local—Pacific Coast from s. British Columbia to Mexican border; inland in s. Manitoba, Dakotas, Washington, Oregon, n. California, n.w. Nevada; winters in s. parts of Arizona, New Mexico, Texas, along Pacific Coast from s. British Columbia to Mexican border.

REDHEAD 20"

Gray body; reddish head; black chest; *rounded* profile; *short* bill. **Habitat:** Lakes, rivers, marshes, bays, estuaries. **Range:** S. Canada to Mexican border; winters north to California, s. Nevada, Utah, Colorado, Kansas.

CANVASBACK 22"

White body; dark chestnut head and neck; black chest; *sloping* profile; *long* bill. **Habitat:** Lakes, rivers, marshes, bays, estuaries. **Range:** S. Canada to Mexican border; winters north to British Columbia, Montana, w. South Dakota.

Plate 39. **DIVING DUCKS 1**

Greater
Scaup

Lesser
Scaup F.

M.

Ring-necked Duck

Redhead

Canvasback

87

Plate 40. **DIVING DUCKS 2**

BUFFLEHEAD 14"

Large white patch on dark head; white body; black back; close-up—iridescent green and purple head; female—small white patch on dark head behind eye; grayish body. **Habitat:** Lakes, rivers, bays, inlets, estuaries. **Range:** S. Canada to Mexican border; winters north to British Columbia, Nevada, s.w. Utah, New Mexico, s.e. Nebraska.

COMMON GOLDENEYE 18"

Dark puffy head; white body; white patch behind bill; black back; close-up—glossy *green* head; bright yellow eye; female—gray body and dark brown head separated by white collar. **Habitat:** Lakes, rivers, bays, inlets, estuaries. **Range:** Pacific Coast from British Columbia to Mexican border; also s.e. California, s.w. Arizona.

BARROW'S GOLDENEYE 18"

White crescent between bill and eye; close-up—glossy *purple* head; black back with row of white spots along side; white below. **Habitat:** Wooded lakes, ponds, rivers; inlets estuaries. **Range:** Pacific Coast from British Columbia to c. California, inland from Washington, Oregon to n. Idaho, w. Montana, n.w. Wyoming; winters south to Utah, Colorado; also s.e. California, s. Arizona.

HOODED MERGANSER 17½"

Fan-shaped white crest with black border; rusty sides; white breast with two vertical black stripes; black face, neck, and back. **Habitat:** Wooded lakes, ponds, streams. **Range:** S. British Columbia to Mexican border; winters inland to n. Idaho, s. Oregon, s.e. California, s.w. Arizona.

RED-BREASTED MERGANSER 23"

Swept-back, double crest; red bill; white collar; rusty chest; black back. **Habitat:** Chiefly coastal waters, including ocean. **Range:** Pacific Coast from British Columbia to Mexican border; also s.e. California, extreme s. Nevada, s.w. Arizona.

COMMON MERGANSER 25"

Dark, glossy green head; red bill; white body; black back; female—duller, with red head. **Habitat:** Lakes, reservoirs, rivers; bays in winter. **Range:** S. Canada to Mexican border; winters north to coast of British Columbia, inland to n.e. Oregon, c. Idaho, Wyoming, Dakotas, rarely to s.e. Saskatchewan, s.w. Manitoba.

Plate 40. **DIVING DUCKS 2**

Bufflehead

M.

F.

F.

M.

Common Goldeneye

Barrow's
Goldeneye

Hooded
Merganser

Red-breasted
Merganser

Common
Merganser

F.

M.

Plate 41. **DIVING DUCKS 3**

RUDDY DUCK 15½"

White cheek; bright blue bill; chestnut body; dark cap; cocks tail up into a fan; female—much duller, white cheek with dark horizontal stripe. **Habitat:** Marshes, ponds, lakes, bays, lagoons, estuaries. **Range:** S. Canada to Mexican border; winters along coast north to British Columbia, but inland only to Arizona, New Mexico, c. Texas.

HARLEQUIN DUCK 16½"

Slate head; blue-gray chest and back; prominent white markings on head and body; chestnut sides; female—dusky brown; *three* white facial patches. **Habitat:** Summer—montane streams in forested areas; winter—rocky coasts. **Range:** S. British Columbia to Washington, n.e. Oregon, c. Idaho, w. Montana, n.w. Wyoming; winters along coast from s. British Columbia to c. California.

BLACK SCOTER 18"

All-black sea duck; large orange knob on black bill. **Habitat:** Ocean, bays, larger lakes, rivers. **Range:** Pacific Coast from British Columbia to Mexican border.

SURF SCOTER 19"

Black sea duck; two white head patches—one on forecrown, one on nape; bill black, white, yellow and reddish. **Habitat:** Ocean, bays, larger lakes, rivers. **Range:** Pacific Coast from British Columbia to Mexican border.

WHITE-WINGED SCOTER 21"

Black sea duck; small white eye patch; larger white wing patch, most evident in flight; orange bill with black basal knob. **Habitat:** Ocean, bays, large lakes, rivers. **Range:** S. Canada to Mexican border; winters along Pacific Coast. **Note:** All three scoters are rare and irregular *inland* in w. United States.

Plate 41. **DIVING DUCKS 3**

Ruddy Duck

F.

M. summer

Harlequin Duck

F.

M.

Black Scoter

Surf Scoter

White-winged Scoter

Plate 42. **ALCIDS, LOONS**

PIGEON GUILLEMOT 13"

Small chunky seabird; pointed bill; mostly black; large white wing patch with triangular black wedge; red feet; winter—white head, neck and below. **Habitat:** Rocky coasts, islands, ocean. **Range:** Pacific Coast from s. British Columbia to Mexican border.

COMMON (THIN-BILLED) MURRE 17"

Stocky seabird; long *slender*, pointed bill; deep sooty brown above, white below; winter—similar, but neck and throat white; black cheek stripe. **Habitat:** Rocky coasts, islands; ocean. **Range:** Pacific Coast from s. British Columbia to Mexican border.

RED-THROATED LOON 25"

Sharp, pointed bill tilted *upward*; nonbreeding plumage—white head, neck, and below. **Habitat:** Ocean, bays, estuaries. **Range:** Pacific Coast from s. British Columbia to Mexican border. **Note:** Rarely seen in breeding plumage (red throat).

PACIFIC LOON 25"

Sharp, pointed, *straight* bill; pearl-gray crown and nape; black throat; conspicuous square white patches on dark back; winter—white cheeks and throat; dark line from eye down side of neck. **Habitat:** Ocean. **Range:** Pacific Coast from s. British Columbia to Mexican border.

COMMON LOON 32"

Large size; long, sharp, pointed, *straight* bill; black head and neck; blotched black-and-white back and sides; winter—white face, neck, and below. **Habitat:** Large wooded lakes, ocean, bays. **Range:** S. Canada, Pacific Coast from Washington to Mexican border; occasionally inland in winter to s.e. California, s.w. Arizona.

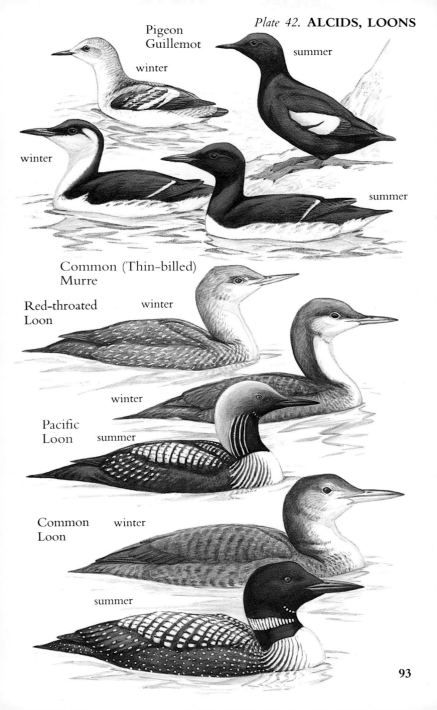

Plate 42. **ALCIDS, LOONS**

Pigeon
Guillemot

winter

summer

winter

summer

Common (Thin-billed)
Murre

Red-throated
Loon

winter

winter

Pacific
Loon

summer

Common
Loon

winter

summer

Plate 43. **GREBES**

PIED-BILLED GREBE 13"

Black ring on thick whitish bill; brownish body with black throat; nonbreeding—similar but *no* black. **Habitat:** Marshes, weedy ponds, lakes; bays in winter. **Range:** S. Canada to Mexican border; winters north to s. British Columbia, Nevada, Utah, s.w. Colorado, s. Kansas.

HORNED GREBE 13½"

Golden ear tufts; black head and back; *chestnut* neck and sides; nonbreeding—black above, white below. **Habitat:** Lakes, ponds, rivers, bays, inlets, ocean. **Range:** Chiefly Pacific Coast from British Columbia to Mexican border; also s. Canada and n. U.S. border states, but in winter only along coast and extreme s. Texas.

EARED GREBE 13"

Golden ear tufts; *black* head, *neck*, chest, and back; chestnut below; nonbreeding—blackish above with white only on chin and small patch behind cheek; thin, upturned bill. **Habitat:** Ponds, lakes, bays, ocean. **Range:** S. Canada to Mexican border; winters along Pacific Coast, inland north to Nevada, Utah, Colorado, c. Texas.

WESTERN GREBE 25"

Our largest grebe; extremely long, swanlike neck; black above, white below; blackish cap extends *below* eye; long, thin, slightly upturned *greenish* bill. **Habitat:** Reedy lakes, ponds; bays, estuaries. **Range:** All of California, most mountain states, s.w. Arizona, s. and w. Texas; winters locally along Pacific coast from s.w. British Columbia to Mexican border; summers in s.e. Saskatchewan, s. Manitoba to Dakotas.

CLARK'S GREBE 25"

Very similar to Western Grebe, but white of cheeks *surrounds* eyes; beak is yellow orange. **Habitat:** Reedy lakes, ponds; bays, estuaries. **Range:** Mostly the same as Western Grebe, but more common in s. portion of range. **Note:** Formerly considered a form of the Western Grebe; now recognized as a distinct species as the two are reported not to interbreed.

Plate 43. **GREBES**

Pied-billed
Grebe

winter

Horned
Grebe

summer

Eared
Grebe

summer

winter

Clark's
Grebe

Western
Grebe

95

Plate 44. **RAILS, GALLINULE, COOT**

SORA 9"

Chickenlike; short, thick yellow bill; black face, throat, and chest; brown above, gray below; narrow white bars on flanks. **Habitat:** Marshes, moist meadows. **Range:** S. Canada to Mexican border; winters north to Washington, s. Nevada, c. Arizona, New Mexico, Texas.

VIRGINIA RAIL 9½"

Chickenlike; long, slender, slightly curved bill; grayish brown above; gray cheeks; rusty below; large chestnut wing patch; narrow white bars on gray flanks. **Habitat:** Marshes. **Range:** Local from s. Canada to Mexican border, c. New Mexico, n. Texas, much of Oklahoma; winters north to Washington, s. Nevada, Arizona, c. New Mexico, lower Gulf coast of s. Texas.

CLAPPER RAIL 15"

Chickenlike; much larger than Virginia Rail; long, slender, slightly curved bill; grayish brown above; cheeks, breast, and underparts rusty; narrow white bars on flanks. **Habitat:** Coastal marshes. **Range:** Local—restricted to c. and s.e. California, s.w. Arizona, Gulf Coast along Texas. **Note:** The nearly identical King Rail inhabits inland freshwater marshes of e. U.S., and also occurs in s. Texas where the two species may hybridize.

COMMON MOORHEN (COMMON GALLINULE) 13"

Bright red forehead and bill with yellow tip; deep gray head and body; olive-brown back; narrow white side stripe. **Habitat:** Marshes, ponds; lawns near water. **Range:** Local—resident from c. California, s.w. Nevada, c. Arizona, c. New Mexico to Mexican border; also Oklahoma, e.c. Texas.

AMERICAN COOT 14½"

Deep gray with *white* bill. **Habitat:** Marshes, ponds, lakes, bays; lawns, fields. **Range:** S. Canada to Mexican border; winters north to s. British Columbia, n.e. Nevada, s. Utah, s. and e. Colorado, most of Nebraska.

Sora

Plate 44. **RAILS, GALLINULE, COOT**

Virginia Rail

Clapper
Rail

Common Moorhen
(Common Gallinule)

American
Coot

97

Plate 45. **CORMORANTS, PELICANS**

BRANDT'S CORMORANT 34"

All black with blue chin pouch, bordered behind with bluff. **Habitat:** Cliffs along rocky seacoasts. **Range:** Pacific Coast from British Columbia to Mexican border.

PELAGIC CORMORANT 27"

Smaller and more slender than other cormorants; all black with green and purple iridescence at close range; white flank patch in breeding adult, evident in flight. **Habitat:** Cliffs along rocky seacoasts. **Range:** Pacific Coast from British Columbia to Mexican border.

DOUBLE-CRESTED CORMORANT 33"

All black with orange chin pouch. **Habitat:** Coastal bays, islands; inland lakes, rivers. **Range:** Resident on Pacific Coast from British Columbia to Mexican border; Rio Grande Valley and Gulf coast of Texas; breeds from s. Canada south through much of inland states to Utah, Colorado, Dakotas, Nebraska, but winters north only to U.S.-Mexico border and Lower Gulf Coast.

BROWN PELICAN 50"

Very large; grayish brown; very long grayish white bill; white head, chestnut neck; immature—dull brownish. **Habitat:** Ocean, bays, inlets, beaches. **Range:** C. California to Mexican border; less common north along coast to Washington.

WHITE PELICAN 62"

Huge white bird; very long orange bill; much black in wings, evident in flight. **Habitat:** Lakes, marshes, shallow bays, coastal estuaries. **Range:** Breeds locally on large inland lakes from s. Canada to Mexican border; winters locally north to c. California, s. Nevada, w. Arizona, extreme s. Texas.

Plate 45. **CORMORANTS, PELICANS**

Pelagic Cormorant

Brandt's
Cormorant

Double-
crested
Cormorant

Brown
Pelican

in flight

White
Pelican

99

Plate 46. **LONG-LEGGED WADERS 1**

CATTLE EGRET 20"

Small, stocky, and thick necked; breeding—golden buff plumes on head, breast, and back; short orange-red bill; reddish legs; nonbreeding-all-white plumage; yellow bill; greenish legs. **Habitat:** Fields, pastures, farms; airports; golf courses, lawns. **Range:** S. portions of California, Arizona, New Mexico; South Dakota to Texas; wanders north to U.S.-Canada border; winters primarily along U.S.-Mexico border and in much of Texas. **Note:** Often associates with cattle and other livestock.

GREAT EGRET 38"

Large; all-white plumage; yellow bill; black legs. **Habitat:** Marshes, swamps, ponds, bays, tidal flats. **Range:** Oregon to Mexican border; s. Arizona, New Mexico; also s.e. Kansas, e.c. Oklahoma to c. Texas; wanders north to U.S.-Canada border; winters north to s.w. Oregon, s. Nevada, s. Arizona, s.w. New Mexico, extreme s. Texas.

SNOWY EGRET 23"

Small, slender; all-white plumage; black bill and legs; yellow feet. **Habitat:** Marshes, swamps, ponds, shallow bays, tidal flats. **Range:** S. parts of Oregon, Idaho, Wyoming to Mexican border, east to c. Colorado, Oklahoma, w. Texas; wanders north to U.S.-Canada border; winters north to n. California, s. Nevada, w. Arizona, extreme s. Texas.

SANDHILL CRANE 45"

Very large; all-gray plumage; bare red crown; black legs. **Habitat:** Prairies, fields, swales, marshes. **Range:** Local from s. Alberta, Saskatchewan to e. Washington, Oregon, n. Nevada, Idaho, w. Montana, Wyoming, extreme n. Utah, Colorado; winters in c. and s.e. California, s. parts of Arizona, New Mexico, w., c., and s. Texas. **Note:** Flies with neck *outstretched*.

GREAT BLUE HERON 44"

Very large; bluish gray; whitish head; black head plumes. **Habitat:** Marshes, swamps, lakes, rivers, bays, estuaries. **Range:** S. Canada to Mexican border; winters north to s. British Columbia, e. Oregon, Nevada, s. Utah, s.w. Colorado, c. Oklahoma. **Note:** Flies with neck *folded in*.

Plate 46. **LONG-LEGGED WADERS 1**

summer

winter

Cattle
Egret

Great
Egret

Snowy
Egret

in flight

Sandhill
Crane

in flight

Great Blue
Heron

101

LEAST BITTERN 13"

Our smallest heron; greenish black above; buff wing patch; tawny sides of head and neck. **Habitat:** Dense marshes, especially those with cattails and tule. **Range:** Local in West—from c. California to Mexican border; s.w. Arizona; from Dakotas south to c. and s.w. Texas; winters chiefly south of border, rarely in s. California, s. Arizona, lower Gulf coast of s. Texas.

AMERICAN BITTERN 23"

Stocky; tawny-brown with dark streaks below—blending with reeds; black neck stripe; blackish outer wings, evident in flight. **Habitat:** Marshes, wet meadows, bogs. **Range:** S. Canada to Mexican border; winters north along Pacific Coast to s.w. British Columbia, inland to s. parts of Nevada, Utah, n. New Mexico, w. and c. Texas.

GREEN HERON 18"

Small and chunky; chestnut head and neck; bluish gray back and wings, the back with green sheen; greenish yellow legs. **Habitat:** Marshes, swamps, wooded ponds, streams, coastal thickets. **Range:** Local from s. Canada to Mexican border; winters north to California, s. Arizona, extreme s. Texas.

BLACK-CROWNED NIGHT-HERON 25"

Stocky; black cap and back; two long white head plumes in breeding season; gray wings; white below; immature—brown, streaked and spotted with white. **Habitat:** Marshes, swamps, wooded ponds, streams, tidal flats. **Range:** Local from s. Canada to Mexican border; winters north to s.w. Oregon, s.w. Arizona, extreme s. Texas.

WHITE-FACED IBIS 24"

Black at distance; slender, decurved bill; close-up—iridescent bronze-green, chestnut, and purple. Very similar to Glossy Ibis of the East, but has *white* border nearly around red eye and red facial skin; reddish bill and legs. **Habitat:** Marshes, swamps, coastal estuaries. **Range:** Local—c. California, s.e. Oregon, Nevada, Utah, e. portions of Rocky Mountain states from s.e. Montana, Dakotas, Colorado, New Mexico, Texas; from Nebraska to e.c. parts of Kansas, Oklahoma; winters in s. Texas, otherwise south of Mexican border.

Plate 47. **LONG-LEGGED WADERS 2**

Least
Bittern

American
Bittern

Green Heron

imm.

Black-crowned
Night-Heron

ad.

White-faced
Ibis

Plate 48. **LARGE SHOREBIRDS**

AMERICAN AVOCET 18"

Flashy black-and-white wings; long, slender, upturned black bill; blue-gray legs; head and neck in breeding plumage—rusty; nonbreeding—pale gray. **Habitat:** Shallow lakes, open marshes, shores, flats. **Range:** S. Alberta, Saskatchewan, Manitoba to Mexican border, east to Dakota, c. Nebraska, w. Kansas, w. Oklahoma, n.w. Texas; winters in w.c. and s.e. California, s. Arizona, extreme s. Texas.

BLACK-NECKED STILT 15"

Black above, white below; long red legs; thin black bill. **Habitat:** Open marshes, shallow lakes, pools; tidal flats and estuaries. **Range:** Local form Oregon, Nevada, Utah, s. Colorado, w.c. Kansas to Mexican border; winters chiefly south of border, but also s. parts of California, Arizona, Texas.

MARBLED GODWIT 18"

Long, slightly upturned bill; tawny-brown body. **Habitat:** Prairies; pools, lake shores; coastal flats, beaches. **Range:** Breeds locally from s. Alberta, Saskatchewan, Manitoba to Montana, Dakotas; migrates throughout much of West; winters chiefly south of U.S.-Mexico border, but also along Pacific coast of California, Gulf coast of Texas.

LONG-BILLED CURLEW 23"

Our largest shorebird; extremely long, decurved bill; cinnamon brown above, tawny-buff below. **Habitat:** Plains, prairies, wet meadows, shores, beaches. **Range:** Local from s. Canada to Mexican border; east to w. Dakotas, n.w. Nebraska, e. Colorado, n.e. New Mexico, Texas; winters locally in California, s.w. Arizona, c. and s. Texas.

WHIMBREL 17"

Long, decurved bill; brown and white head stripes; gray-brown body. **Habitat:** Shores, flats, prairies, wet meadows. **Range:** Breeds locally in high Arctic; migrates nearly throughout; winters chiefly in tropics, but also along Pacific coast of California, Gulf coast of Texas.

Plate 48. **LARGE SHOREBIRDS**

American
Avocet

summer

Black-
necked
Stilt

Marbled
Godwit

Long-billed
Curlew

Whimbrel

Plate 49. **MEDIUM SHOREBIRDS**

SPOTTED SANDPIPER 7½"

Breeding—black spots below; nonbreeding—plain white below; white wedge in front of wing; rear end teeters up and down; in flight, flutters stiffly held, downcurved wings. **Habitat:** Shores of ponds, streams, often on logs, rocks; beaches, dunes. **Range:** S. Canada to Mexican border; winters along West Coast north to Washington, inland to c. California, s. Arizona, s. New Mexico, c. Texas.

UPLAND SANDPIPER 12"

Tawny-brown; thin neck; long tail; yellowish legs. **Habitat:** Shortgrass prairies, hayfields, meadows, pastures; airports; often perches on poles, fence posts. **Range:** Very local—breeds from s. Alberta, Saskatchewan, Manitoba; from e. Washington, Idaho, Montana, North Dakota to e. Wyoming, south to n.e. Colorado, n.w. Oklahoma; migrates mainly through w. plains, prairies; winters in South America.

COMMON SNIPE 11"

Extremely long bill; striped head and back; tawny-orange tail, evident in flight. **Habitat:** Bogs, marshes, flooded fields, meadows. **Range:** S. Canada to Mexican border; winters north along w. coast to s. British Columbia, inland to s.e. Oregon, s. Idaho, Colorado, n.e. New Mexico, c. Texas.

LONG-BILLED DOWITCHER 11" to 12"

Extremely long bill; breeding—rusty red breast with black spots; sides with bars; nonbreeding—dull gray; white eye stripe; all year—conspicuous white rump wedge, evident in flight. **Habitat:** Tidal flats, muddy shores, open marshes, grassy pools, lagoons. **Range:** Breeds in far north; migrates along West Coast, inland from s. Canada to Mexican border; winters north along coast to British Columbia, inland along U.S.-Mexico border, Gulf Coast. **Note:** Feeds in mud and fairly deep water, using its long bill in "sewing-machine" rhythm.

GREATER YELLOWLEGS 14"

Bright yellow legs; long bill; bobs up and down; white rump in flight. **Habitat:** Tidal flats, marshes, lake and river shores, flooded fields; golf courses. **Range:** S. Canada to Mexican border; migrates throughout; winters north along coast to Washington, inland to s. Nevada, c. Arizona, n.e. New Mexico, w. and s. Texas.

WILLET 15"

Flashy black-and-white wings in flight; bluish gray legs; breeding—speckled body; nonbreeding—pale gray, unmarked. **Habitat:** Marshes, meadows, tidal flats, shores, beaches. **Range:** S. Canada to Mexican border; migrates throughout; winters along Pacific and Gulf Coasts, north to Oregon.

Plate 49. **MEDIUM SHOREBIRDS**

Spotted
Sandpiper

winter

summer

Upland
Sandpiper

Common
Snipe

Long-billed
Dowitcher

winter

Greater
Yellowlegs

Willet

winter

in flight

Plate 50. **SMALL SHOREBIRDS**

WESTERN SANDPIPER 6½"

Black legs; bill with slight droop at tip; reddish feathers at bend of wing (scapulars). **Habitat:** Shores, mudflats, beaches. **Range:** Breeds in high Arctic; migrates throughout; winters north along Pacific Coast to n. California, inland to s.w. Arizona, Gulf coast of s. Texas.

LEAST SANDPIPER 5½"

Our smallest shorebird; greenish yellow legs; heavily streaked breast. **Habitat:** Grassy mudflats, pools, march edges. **Range:** Breeds in high Arctic; migrates throughout; winters north to coast of Oregon, inland to s. Nevada, c. parts of Arizona, New Mexico, Texas.

DUNLIN 8½"

Bill droops at tip; breeding—black patch on belly; reddish back; non-breeding—grayish brown above, whitish below. **Habitat:** Tidal flats, shores, beaches. **Range:** Breeds in high Arctic; migrates mainly along coast, less common inland; winters north along coast to British Columbia, inland to s.w. Arizona, Gulf coast of extreme s. Texas.

SANDERLING 7½"

Breeding—rusty head, back, and breast; nonbreeding—our palest sandpiper, appearing almost white in flight. **Habitat:** Ocean beaches, sand flats, shores. **Range:** Breeds in high Arctic; migrates throughout, but most prevalent along both coasts; winters north along Pacific Coast to British Columbia, Gulf coast of Texas. **Note:** Frequents outer sand beaches, running in and out of waves.

RED KNOT 10½"

Greenish legs; breeding—brick red below; nonbreeding—gray above, whitish below. **Habitat:** Tidal flats, shores, beaches, salt meadows. **Range:** Breeds in high Arctic; migrates chiefly along coasts, much less common inland; winters north to c. California, extreme s. Texas.

WILSON'S PHALAROPE 9"

Long, thin, needlelike bill; breeding—black stripe through eye, extending down neck; cinnamon below black stripe, curving to back; pale gray crown and nape; nonbreeding—combination of white rump in flight and pale unmarked wings and body. **Habitat:** Shallow lakes, ponds; marshes; shortgrass flats. **Range:** Breeds from s. Canada to c. California, Nevada, Utah, Colorado, w. Kansas; migrates throughout; winters in South America.

RED-NECKED PHALAROPE 8"

Breeding-chestnut sides and front of neck; white throat; mostly gray above; nonbreeding—pale gray and white with prominent black patch behind eye; striped back. **Habitat:** Coastal lagoons, estuaries; less numerous on inland lakes. **Range:** Breeds in high Arctic; migrates along coasts, much less numerous inland; winters at sea. **Note:** Phalaropes frequently spin around in the water.

Plate 50. **SMALL SHOREBIRDS**

Western Sandpiper

Least Sandpiper

winter

Dunlin

winter

summer

summer

Sanderling

winter

summer

Red Knot

summer

Wilson's Phalarope

Red-necked Phalarope

winter

winter

109

Plate 51. **ROCK-LOVING SHOREBIRDS**

RUDDY TURNSTONE 9"

Orange legs; breeding—striking black, white, and reddish plumage; nonbreeding—much duller, brownish above, white below with dark breast patch. **Habitat:** Rocky shores, islands, pebbly beaches, tidal flats, salt meadows. **Range:** Breeds in high Arctic; migrates chiefly along coasts, rare in interior; winters north to s.w. Oregon; extreme s. Texas.

BLACK TURNSTONE 9"

Blackish legs; mostly black, with white belly; striking black-and-white wing and tail pattern, evident in flight. **Habitat:** Rocky shores, jetties, pebbly beaches, flats. **Range:** On the coast from British Columbia to Mexican border.

SURFBIRD 10"

Stocky with heavy, short bill; slaty above; paler breast and whitish belly; greenish legs; in flight, striking white rump and base of tail, with black triangular tail band. Far northern breeder; only non-breeding (winter) plumage shown. **Habitat:** Rocky shores, jetties. **Range:** Winters on Pacific Coast from s. British Columbia to Mexican border.

ROCK SANDPIPER 8½"

Dark bill with light base, slightly downcurved; nonbreeding—slaty above; pale gray breast, white belly; greenish yellow legs. **Habitat:** Rocky shores, jetties. **Range:** Winters on Pacific Coast from s. British Columbia to n. California. **Note:** Similar in appearance and habitat to Purple Sandpiper of Atlantic Coast.

WANDERING TATTLER 11"

Uniform slaty above, paler below; yellowish legs; in flight, *no* markings on solid gray wings or tail. Far northern breeder; only non-breeding (winter) plumage shown. **Habitat:** Rocky shores, jetties. **Range:** Migrates along Pacific Coast from s. British Columbia to Mexican border; winters north to s. California, rarely farther.

BLACK OYSTERCATCHER 17½"

Large; all-black plumage; heavy red bill; flesh-colored legs. **Habitat:** Rocky coasts, island, stone jetties. **Range:** Resident along Pacific Coast from s. British Columbia to Mexican border.

Plate 51. **ROCK-LOVING SHOREBIRDS**

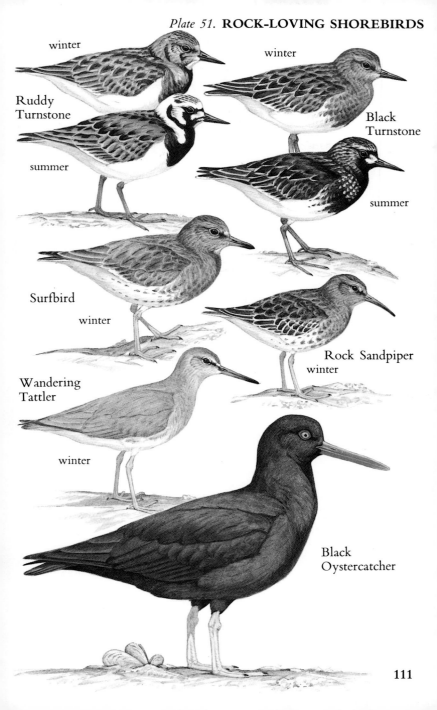

winter

winter

Ruddy
Turnstone

Black
Turnstone

summer

summer

Surfbird

winter

Rock Sandpiper

winter

Wandering
Tattler

winter

Black
Oystercatcher

Plate 52. **MORE SHOREBIRDS—PLOVERS**

SEMIPALMATED PLOVER 7"

Single black breast band; dark above, white below; yellow bill with black tip; yellow legs. **Habitat:** Mudflats, beaches, lake and river shores. **Range:** Breeds in high Arctic; migrates throughout; winters along coasts, north to c. California, s. Texas.

SNOWY PLOVER 6½"

No breast band; dark patches on sides of neck; pale above, white below; thin black bill; slaty legs. **Habitat:** Sand beaches, flats; alkaline lake and river shores. **Range:** Local along Pacific Coast from s.w. Washington to Mexican border; inland from s. Oregon to s.e. California, s. Arizona, s.e. New Mexico, and from s.w. to n.c. Kansas, Gulf Coast, and s. Texas.

KILLDEER 10"

Two black breast bands; brown above, white below; tawny-orange rump, evident in flight. **Habitat:** Short-grass and plowed fields, airports; golf courses; lake and river shores. **Range:** S. Canada to Mexican border; winters on coast north to British Columbia, inland to n. California, s. Nevada, Arizona, New Mexico, Oklahoma, s.e. Kansas.

MOUNTAIN PLOVER 9"

Dark above, white below—our only plover that is *unmarked* below. **Habitat:** Semiarid country on high plains, plateaus, short-grass fields, barren desert flats—often far from water. **Range:** Breeds locally from s. Alberta, Saskatchewan through Montana, Wyoming, Colorado, n.e. New Mexico, more rarely to w. portions of Nebraska, Kansas, Oklahoma, Texas; winters from Mexican border north to California, s. Arizona, extreme s. Texas.

AMERICAN GOLDEN-PLOVER 10½"

Breeding—all black below, dark above with golden spangles; white extending from forehead to eyebrows, and down neck; nonbreeding—dark above, lighter below; *dark* rump. **Habitat:** Prairies; short-grass, plowed fields. **Range:** Breeds in high Arctic; migrates throughout; winters in s. South America.

BLACK-BELLIED PLOVER 12"

Breeding—black below with white vent; mottled gray and white above; white forehead, over and behind eye, and down neck; nonbreeding—whitish below; *white* rump, evident in flight. **Habitat:** Tidal flats, salt meadows, shores; plowed fields, golf courses, large lawns. **Range:** Breeds in high Arctic; migrates throughout; winters along Pacific Coast from British Columbia to Mexican border; lower Gulf coast of Texas.

Plate 52. **MORE SHOREBIRDS—PLOVERS**

Semipalmated
Plover

Snowy Plover

Killdeer

Mountain
Plover

American
Golden-Plover

winter

summer

Black-bellied
Plover

winter

summer

113

Plate 53. **LARGE AND MEDIUM GULLS**

MEW GULL 17"

Pale gray back and wings; *all-yellow, unmarked* bill; greenish yellow legs. **Habitat:** Coasts, beaches, bays, flats. **Range:** Pacific Coast from British Columbia to Mexican border; winters throughout, but breeds only in Canadian portion.

HEERMANN'S GULL 19"

White head and neck, in contrast with slate gray body; lighter below; *red* bill; *blackish* legs. **Habitat:** Rocky coasts, islands, beaches, bays, inlets, estuaries. **Range:** Breeds south of Mexican border (Baja California); ranges *after* breeding season *north* to c. California; in nonbreeding season, wanders to Puget Sound, Washington, Vancouver Island.

RING-BILLED GULL 19"

Pale gray back and wings; yellow bill with *black band;* yellow legs. **Habitat:** Lakes, rivers, beaches, bays, flooded and plowed fields; airports; golf courses, large lawns; refuse dumps, even municipal parking lots for food scraps. **Range:** S. Canada to Mexican border, inland south and east to Great Basin, Dakotas; winters north to s. British Columbia, s.e. Nevada, s.w. Utah, w. and s. Arizona, s.w. New Mexico, s. Texas, northeast to e. Kansas.

CALIFORNIA GULL 21"

Pale gray back and wings; yellow bill with red and black spots; greenish yellow legs. **Habitat:** Ocean beaches, lakes, rivers, marshes; farms; cities, piers. **Range:** S. Canada along Pacific Coast to Mexican border, inland to Great Basin, east to Dakotas; winters along coast to s. British Columbia, inland to s.e. California, s.w. Arizona.

HERRING GULL 24"

Pale gray back and wings; yellow bill with red spot; pinkish legs. **Habitat:** Ocean beaches, lakes, rivers, harbors, piers, flooded fields; golf courses; refuse dumps. **Range:** Local in West, breeds in Arctic Canada; migrates throughout; winters from s. British Columbia to Mexican border, inland east to Idaho, much of California; also e. parts of Texas, Oklahoma, Kansas.

WESTERN GULL 25"

Dark gray back and wings; yellow bill with red spot; pinkish legs. **Habitat:** Rocky cliffs, islets; sand beaches, mudflats, bays, estuaries. **Range:** Resident on Pacific Coast from s. British Columbia to Mexican border.

GLAUCOUS-WINGED GULL 25"

Pale gray back and wings *(including wing tips);* yellow bill with red spot; pinkish legs. **Habitat:** Ocean beaches, bays, piers, dumps. **Range:** Breeds on Pacific Coast from s.w. British Columbia to n.w. Oregon; winters from s. British Columbia to Mexican border.

Plate 53. LARGE AND MEDIUM GULLS

Mew Gull

Heermann's Gull

Ring-billed Gull

California Gull

imm. in flight

Herring Gull

ad.

Western Gull

Glaucous-winged Gull

Plate 54. **SMALL GULLS, TERNS**

FRANKLIN'S GULL 14"

Breeding—black hood; dark gray back and wings; *red* bill; dark red legs; wing tips black with white fore and aft, most evident in flight; non-breeding—same, except head mainly whitish with dark patch behind eye, extending onto nape. **Habitat:** Inland prairies, marshes, lakes, sloughs. **Range:** Restricted mainly to w.c. North America, breeding from s. Alberta, Saskatchewan, Manitoba to s.e. Oregon, Idaho, n.w. Utah, n.w. Wyoming, Dakotas; migrates mainly through interior states, i.e., Great Basin, Rockies, w. plains; winters chiefly in w. South America.

BONAPARTE'S GULL 13"

Light gray back and wings; *black* bill; bright red legs; wing tips with white wedge, noticeable in flight; breeding—black hood; nonbreeding—same, except white head with dark spot behind eye. **Habitat:** Ocean, bays, lakes, rivers. **Range:** Breeds from s. Canada northward; migrates throughout; winters—Pacific Coast north to Washington, s.w. Arizona to Gulf Coast.

LEAST TERN 9"

Breeding—yellow bill with black tip; yellow legs; black cap with white forehead; nonbreeding—black bill; mainly white cap. **Habitat:** Ocean beaches, inlets, bays; sandbars in large rivers. **Range:** Breeds along Pacific Coast from c. California to Mexican border, lower Gulf coast of s. Texas; inland on larger rivers (Colorado, Red, Missouri, Mississippi); winters mainly in tropics.

BLACK TERN 9½"

Breeding—black bill and body; gray wings and tail; nonbreeding—similar, but with pied head, white below. **Habitat:** Inland marshes, lakes, ponds, sluggish rivers; fall migration—seacoasts, ocean. **Range:** Breeds inland from s. Canada to c. California, Nevada, Utah, Colorado, Kansas; migrates throughout; winters in tropics.

FORSTER'S TERN 14"

Breeding—orange-red bill with black tip; black cap; nonbreeding—black bill; white head with black patch through eye. **Habitat:** Marshes, lakes, rivers, coasts. **Range:** Breeds inland and on coast from s. Canada to s. California, Nevada, Utah, Colorado, c. Kansas; migrates throughout; winters north to c. California, s. Arizona, s. Texas.

ELEGANT TERN 17"

Slender bill. **Habitat:** Sandy beaches, bays, estuaries. **Range:** Breeds on Pacific coast of Mexico north to s. California; wanders n. to c. portions.

CASPIAN TERN 21"

Our largest tern; *red* bill; slightly forked tail. **Habitat:** Lakes, rivers, beaches, bays, coastal flats, lagoons. **Range:** Breeds from Washington to Mexican border, from s. Canada to Nevada, Utah, Wyoming, Dakotas; lower Gulf coast of Texas; winters north to s. California, Arizona, s. Texas.

summer

Plate 54. **SMALL GULLS, TERNS**

Franklin's
Gull

winter

summer

winter

Bonaparte's
Gull

Least
Tern

winter

Black
Tern

winter

Forster's
Tern

summer

summer

Elegant
Tern

Caspian
Tern

Further Comments
on the Plates

Plates 1 and 2—**Reddish, Birds, Reddish/Orange Birds**
With the exception of the two orange orioles, all of the others are bright red or have some amounts of red in their plumage. Of the eight species that are finchlike, all have heavy bills for cracking seeds. The two tanagers and both orioles are mainly fruit and insect eaters. The one flycatcher, as its name suggests, feeds entirely on insects but is placed here because of its bright red color. The closely related Northern Cardinal and Pyrrhuloxia have *crests.*

Plate 3—**Yellowish Birds**
All of the birds on this plate either are mostly yellow or have some yellow in their plumage. These birds are solidly colored with conspicuous bars or patches on their wings, with the exception of the heavily streaked Pine Siskin.

Plates 4 and 5—**Warblers**
These plates feature a large family of active and mostly brightly colored small birds with slender bills. The one notable exception, the Yellow-breasted Chat, is much larger. The warblers are misnamed, as many of them do not warble at all but instead have buzzy, insectlike notes. Others, such as the Common Yellowthroat, have more distinctive and/or attractive songs.

As with most of the other birds in this volume, the plates show the warblers in their readily identifiable plumages, i.e., spring and summer males in bright breeding dress. Many, but not all, warblers have some yellow in them, and in these two plates, fourteen out of seventeen species do.

Nearly all of these warblers possess one or two distinctive field marks that readily separate them from one another. For example, the Common Yellowthroat has a conspicuous black mask. Two other species are instantly recognized by bright red areas—the Painted Redstart and the Red-faced Warbler.

The following important questions about field marks should be answered when identifying warblers:

1. Does it have either wing bars or wing patches?
2. Does it lack these marks?
3. Is it streaked below?
4. Is it without streaks?
5. Is it yellow or mainly yellow below?
6. Is it white or mainly white below?
7. Does it have conspicuous black markings anywhere about the head, body, or tail?

Plate 6—**Greenish/Grayish Birds**

The two birds at the top of this plate are nearly a small as hummingbirds and are known as kinglets. They are related to the Old World warblers and are extremely active and restless—flitting about continuously. Both kinglets have prominent head markings, the Ruby-crowned with an eye *ring,* the Golden-crowned with an eye *stripe.*

The four vireos are relatively sluggish, thick-billed birds, quite unlike the active, restless, and slender-billed warblers, which they superficially resemble. Both the Gray and Cassin's (Solitary) Vireos have wing bars and eye *rings,* whereas the Red-eyed and the Warbling *lack* wing bars and possess eye stripes.

Plate 7—**Flycatchers**

Flycatchers' behavior is unique. They fly out from a perch for an insect and almost invariably return to the same perch. The upright stance of these birds is also a good means of identification.

Some things to remember: Of the eight flycatcher species on this plate, both the Western Kingbird and the Ash-throated Flycatcher have a gray throat and chest with yellow breast and belly; the Black Phoebe and the Eastern Kingbird are black and white; Say's Phoebe has a cinnamon belly; the Pacific-slope (Western) Flycatcher has an olive breast and a yellowish belly; finally, both the Olive-sided Flycatcher and the Western Wood-Pewee are drab and somber. Check color plate and text for details.

Plates 8 and 9—**Grayish Birds**

As the two plates indicate, these birds either are predominantly gray or have a certain amount of gray in their plumage. The species shown on Plate 8 are much larger than those on Plate 9. The Scissor-tailed Flycatcher may be easily identified by its long, scissorlike tail. The short-tailed American Dipper is always found actively flitting about mountain streams, either on the rocks or in the water. Superficially, it looks like a large, overgrown wren.

The Gray Jay, Clark's Nutcracker, and Townsend's Solitaire are confined mostly to mountains or the North, whereas the Loggerhead Shrike, Northern Mockingbird, and Scissor-tailed Flycatcher are mainly southern in range.

The small birds on Plate 9 consist of two families: the uppermost are gnatcatchers with longish tails; the others are titmice and chickadees, two of which are crested. The three chickadees lack crests, as do the Verdin and the Bushtit. Most of these birds are very tame and can be studied at close range.

Plate 10—**Bluish Birds**

The five birds on this plate represent two different families: the jays and the kingfishers, which are totally unrelated. The Belted Kingfisher, as its name suggests, feeds exclusively on fish. The jays are omnivorous, eating nuts, seeds, fruit, suit, and even bird eggs on occasion.

Three of these five birds are similar in that they possess crests—two of the jays having pointed ones, the Kingfisher a bushy-shaped crest. The remaining two species—the Western Scrub-Jay and the Pinyon Jay—are uncrested. The Blue Jay and the Steller's Jay are in the same genus and are closely related.

Plate 11—**Bluish/Reddish Birds**

The seven birds on this plate are among the brightest colored species anywhere in this field guide. The Painted Bunting, especially, might be described as gaudy, and the Lazuli Bunting and both bluebirds are not far behind; yet, the Blue Grosbeak and both the Indigo and Varied Buntings—bright as they are in full sunlight—appear black at a distance or in poor light.

The five species at the top of this plate are finches, with heavy bills adapted for husking hard-shelled nuts and sunflower seeds. The two bluebirds are members of the thrush family and have slender bills suitable for eating soft-bodied insects and fruits.

Plates 12 to 14—**Sparrows**

The birds on these three plates may be grouped into two main categories: The first category includes the mostly grayish sparrows on Plate 12 and the generally brownish sparrows on Plates 13 and 14.

The second category includes birds that are completely streaked above and below (the Fox, Song, Savannah, and Vesper Sparrows) and those that are completely unstreaked above and below (the three juncos and the Black-throated Sparrow on Plate 12).

All of the remaining sparrows are either unstreaked below or, in the case of the Harris' and Sage Sparrows, partially streaked. Study these birds carefully according to these categories and then progress to each species for its outstanding field marks, given on the text pages opposite the color plates.

Plates 15 to 17—**Brownish Birds**

The six wrens on Plate 15 are small to medium sized and noted for their active and restless habits, as well as for the frequent cocking-up of their tails. The unrelated but somewhat similar-looking Wrentit of the West Coast also cocks its tail, but is more secretive than the wrens, often hiding in scrub and bushes.

The wrens are confined mainly to special habitats. The familiar House Wren is found near buildings, Bewick's Wren in thickets and hedgerows, the Marsh Wren—as its name implies—in cattail marshes and wet reedy places. The remaining three species—as *their* names specify—occur in much drier areas, among rocks and in canyons. The largest of the wrens is found mainly in cactus deserts. All but the Marsh Wren frequent feeders on occasion.

The eight birds on Plate 16 belong to two different families. The towhees are mainly ground-dwelling, sparrowlike birds that feed chiefly on seeds. The four thrashers inhabit brush and thickets, and they superficially resemble thrushes. As can be seen by their slender and somewhat decurved bills, their diet is more varied—berries, insects, and some seeds. All eight species may be found in arid regions, although both the California Towhee and the California Thrasher also dwell in towns and gardens.

The five thrushes and two unrelated waxwings on Plate 17 have one thing in common—they all feed on fruit and insects. The very familiar and versatile American Robin is, of course, best known for its preference for lawns and golf courses and for its consumption of earthworms. Unlike this well-known and conspicuous bird, the beautiful Varied Thrush is much more retiring and lives mostly in humid northwestern forests; in bad winter weather, however, it may be observed at feeders. The three brown-backed thrushes are also relatively shy, but they can be seen in the open if the observer is quiet and cautious.

The two waxwings often occur in large flocks, especially in winter, when they may be readily observed in berry-bearing trees and bushes. They are at times extraordinarily tame and can be approached at close range. In the warmer months, when they pair off and feed extensively on insects, they may be watched at leisure flycatching near wooded ponds and streams. Waxwings are sleek and handsome and are the only birds on these three plates that are crested.

Plate 18—**Grassland Birds**
The seven birds on this plate, belonging to four different families, comprise a miscellaneous assortment of predominantly brownish birds living in open grasslands. The largest bird—the Western Meadowlark—has a short tail, and a black V or chevron across its bright yellow breast. The smaller, similar-looking Horned Lark and Dickcissel are unrelated, as are the tail-wagging American (Water) Pipit and the distinctive winter bird, the Snow Bunting. Finally, the two longspurs are found in grasslands, the Lapland being a winter visitor from the high Arctic tundra.

Plates 19 and 20—**Blackish Birds**
Five different families are represented on these two plates. The crested Phainopepla is a member of the waxwing group; the Lark Bunting is a finch; the European Starling is an Old World bird; the American (Black-billed) Magpie, the American Crow, and the Common Raven belong to the family Corvidae; the Bobolink, the two cowbirds, the three blackbirds, and both grackles are all members of the family Icteridae.

Although many of the above are entirely black or blackish with iridescent plumage, a few have other colors, such as the Yellow-headed Blackbird; the Bobolink with buff and white in breeding plumage; and the American (Black-billed) Magpie, with much white.

Many of these birds inhabit open country, such as marshes, grass-lands, and even deserts, but the Common Raven lives in forested regions, and open, arid areas. The American Crow is found everywhere.

*Plate 21—***Tree Clingers**

The birds on this plate have one thing in common—they spend much of their time on trees. The Brown Creeper and the four wood-peckers forage on the tree trunks and branches by climbing *up*. The three nuthatches, on the other hand, descend head *down*.

The larger White-breasted Nuthatch feeds chiefly on the trunks and large branches of the deciduous hardwoods, while the two smaller species are found in conifers, mainly among the small branches and even probing the cones at the tips of the evergreens.

The Brown Creeper is almost always observed spiraling up a tree, its dull-brown back blending in with the bark; its decurved bill is distinctive.

The four woodpeckers on this plate and the twelve species on Plates 22 and 23 are discussed in detail below.

*Plates 22 and 23—***Woodpeckers**

Including the four species on Plate 21, there are sixteen woodpeckers in all, ranging in size from the spectacular crow-sized, crested Pileated Woodpecker to the very small Downy Woodpecker.

These birds are most frequently seen in an upright position on the trunk of a tree or on a utility pole. With their chisel-shaped bills and stiffly pointed tails, they climb in search of boring insects. The exception is the familiar Northern Flicker, which often feeds on the ground in pursuit of ants.

Most woodpeckers have black–and–white patterns of some sort, either in patches, stripes and bars, or spots. They usually have some red on the head. Only the Red-headed Woodpecker and the male Red-breasted Sapsucker have an entirely red head.

The familiar Downy Woodpecker and the Hairy Woodpecker are replicas of each other, the latter being the larger of the two species.

Most unusual, perhaps, is the great difference between the sexes of the Williamson's Sapsucker. The male is solid black and white with a red throat and yellow belly, whereas the female has a brown head and a zebra–patterned back, tail, and sides. The female was once even described as a different species until, many years later, it was found breeding with the male.

Plate 24—**Swallows**

These graceful aerialists are adept at catching flying insects on the wing and are most often seen in flight. Nevertheless, they may also be observed perched on overhead wires in long rows and, at times, they can be approached at fairly close range. At these roadside gatherings, as many as seven species may be observed on rare occasions. Their differences in size, shape, pattern, and color will be readily noticed.

The Purple Martin, our largest swallow, is the only species in this family in our area that is represented by different-looking sexes. The male is uniformly dark and glossy blue-black; the female is dark above, pale gray below.

Most of our swallows have tails that are either slightly forked or notched. The closely related Barn and Cliff Swallows, however, have tails of vastly different shape: the former's is deeply forked and the latter's is square.

These characteristics are of great importance in separating the different species, either in flight or at rest.

Plate 25—**Swifts, Nightjars**

All three swifts and one of the two nightjars included on this plate are strictly western species. The members of these two families are exclusively aerial insect feeders, and the observer rarely sees them except when they are in flight.

Swifts live up to their name, being among the fastest flying of all birds. Only the White-throated Swift is bicolored, having a conspicuous black-and-white pattern.

Of the two nightjars, the familiar Common Nighthawk may be easily recognized by the prominent white bands on its long, pointed wings. The smaller Common Poorwill, on the other hand, has no white markings on its short, rounded wings. Moreover, it is seen much less frequently than the Common Nighthawk.

Plate 26—**Hummingbirds**

Often called "winged jewels," these smallest of all birds are well represented in the West. Eight of more than sixteen species are depicted here. All occur north of Mexico, the majority being found in southern Arizona, mostly during the summer months.

Only males are shown on the color plate, with the exception of the Black-chinned Hummingbird (both sexes illustrated). This species is the western representative of the familiar Ruby-throated Hummingbird, the only member of the family found in the East. Whereas the drab females look much alike, the glittering males may be told apart by carefully noting the gorget (throat) color and head marking. This is best done when these birds are either perched on a twig or feeding among the flowers.

Plate 27—Cuckoo, Pigeons

The one cuckoo on this plate ranges widely. Seven species of pigeons and doves are represented. The distinction between pigeons and doves is one of size only—the former being larger, the latter generally smaller, although there is some overlap. The largest is the Band-tailed Pigeon at about 15 inches; the smallest is the sparrow-sized Common Ground-Dove at about 6½ inches.

The most widespread of this group is the familiar and numerous Mourning Dove. The most restricted is the introduced Spotted Dove (from Asia), now well established in southern California. Introduced from Europe, the semidomesticated Rock (Dove) Pigeon is well known to urban and suburban dwellers.

Plates 28 and 29—Game Birds

These birds are all chickenlike, with the Northern Bobwhite the smallest, the Wild Turkey the largest.

Unlike the eastern guide, which has only one plate and four species of game birds, the western guide has two plates and fourteen species. Moreover, all four eastern game birds are repeated in the current volume, plus *ten* all-western game birds. The two plates are divided into the smaller game birds and the larger ones. The first plate consists of five quails (the Northern Bobwhite is a quail) and two partridges—both introduced from Eurasia. The second plate includes the Wild Turkey, the Ring-necked Pheasant—introduced from western Asia—and four kinds of grouse.

The last species is included here with the game birds, as it has the appearance of being chickenlike. However, it is actually a large ground cuckoo—the well-known and conspicious Greater Roadrunner of the southwestern deserts.

Plates 30 to 33—**Hawks**

Nineteen species of hawklike birds or diurnal raptors appear on these four plates. They consist of two vultures, two eagles, five buteos, two accipiters, the Osprey and the Northern Harrier (Marsh Hawk), two kites, and four falcons.

Many of these species occur from coast to coast or nearly so. The Swainson's and Ferruginous Hawks and the Prairie Falcon are exclusively western in distribution. The Golden Eagle is quite common in the West but rare and local in the East. The Black Vulture and Mississippi Kite, however, are mostly southeastern in range, while the Red-shouldered Hawk is mainly an eastern species, with an isolated population in California. Finally, the White-tailed Kite is restricted to the Pacific coastal areas of Oregon and California; also the Gulf coast of Texas.

The most important clue in hawk identification is the shape of the wings and tail, especially noticeable in overhead flight; distinctive also is the manner of flight. The plates accompanying text emphasize patterns and colors, especially when these birds are perched, sometimes at close range. Only adults are illustrated, unless otherwise noted.

Plates 34 and 35—**Owls**

The ten species of owls on these two plates range from the Great Horned Owl, which is as large as a Red-tailed Hawk—both nearly 2 feet in length—to the world's smallest owl, the tiny Elf Owl, as small as a sparrow (6 inches).

Only two of these ten species have dark eyes—the Barn Owl and the Spotted Owl—imparting a "mild" appearance; the remaining species have light-colored, yellowish eyes, which give them a somewhat "fierce" expression.

Three owls possess head tufts—the Great Horned, Long-eared, and Western Screech-Owls. Their head tufts are strictly ornamental and have nothing to do with hearing. The other seven species are tuftless, although the Short-eared Owl, as its name implies, has tiny head tufts, not visible in the field.

With the exception of the Burrowing and Short-eared Owls, both of which are open-country and ground-dwelling species, owls inhabit tree groves and dense forests. The Barn and Great Horned Owls, however, sometimes nest on cliffs or among rocks.

All owls have large heads and appear to have no neck.

Plate 36—**Geese, Swans**

There are many white birds, but in our part of the world, few are as large as a swan. Swans are much larger than geese and have longer necks. When they are in flight, they look enormous, with head and outstretched neck as long as the body!

Both species of swans have twice the bulk of Snow Geese. In addition to being completely white, including their wing tips, the two western swans have *black* bills, whereas Snow Geese possess conspicuous black wing tips and have *pink* bills.

The biggest problem for beginners lies in distinguishing geese from ducks. As a rule, geese have longer necks than ducks (which is how swans differ from geese). Geese are generally larger, and their bodies are heavier. The Brant (a goose) is the exception: it is Mallard sized.

Finally, geese are frequently seen grazing on land, particularly in fields and on golf courses. Ducks and swans are more partial to water and are most often observed swimming.

Plates 37 to 41—**Ducks**

For many birders, ducks are difficult to identify in flight, except after long experience. For this reason, the illustrations show them only on water or land, where one has the best opportunity to identify them.

As you go through the plates, you will notice that ducks are grouped as follows:

Plates 37 and 38—Tipping Ducks. These ducks feed mostly in shallow water by tipping and upending on or near the surface of the water; they also forage on land.

Plates 39 to 41—Diving Ducks. These ducks chiefly inhabit deep water, where they feed by diving from the surface; they obtain much of their food at or near the bottom.

As for color differences, ducks may also be grouped according to whether their heads are all or mostly green; for example, the Mallard, the Northern Shoveler, and both the common and the red-breasted mergansers all have green heads. Within this group there are also marked differences. The Mallard has a white ring around its neck, the Northern Shoveler has a spoon-shaped bill, one of the two mergansers is crested, and both have long red bills.

One might also categorize ducks by various conspicuous white patches on the head, wings, or body. Many have prominent white markings—the Northern Pintail, the American Wigeon (Baldpate), the Northern Shoveler, the Blue-winged Teal, the Ruddy Duck, the Black-bellied Whistling-Duck, the Canvasback, the Surf Scoter, the two goldeneyes, the Bufflehead, and all three mergansers.

Finally, the tipping ducks are found chiefly on sheltered ponds, marshes, and wooded swamps, whereas the deep-water diving ducks frequent large lakes and reservoirs, coastal bays and estuaries, and the ocean itself, albeit close to shore.

Plate 42—**Alcids, Loons**

Loons are black-and-white goose-sized divers with short, thick necks and short, pointed bills. On the water, loons can be distinguished from cormorants by the position of their bills—bills of loons point straight ahead, those of cormorants slant upward.

Both the Pigeon Guillemot and the Common (Thin-billed) Murre are members of the alcid family—black-and-white ducklike seabirds, but with pointed bills. This primarily far-northern family includes auks, murres, guillemots, and puffins, among others. When nesting, they inhabit rocky shores and cliffs.

Plate 43—**Grebes**

Grebes, loonlike with lobbed feet, sit low in the water, appear to be tailless, and have daggerlike bills. They are, therefore, easily distinguished from ducks. The small Pied-billed Grebe, however, has a thick, chickenlike bill. The very large Western and Clark's Grebes may be identified easily by their long, gleaming white necks, which have a swanlike curve.

All grebes, when diving from the surface, sink into the water and reappear at another spot.

Plate 44—**Rails, Gallinule, Coot**

The American Coot and the Common Moorhen (Common Gallinule) are ducklike birds with chickenlike bills. The white bill contrasting with the dark gray body is a sure sign of the Coot, and the red, yellow-tipped bill is a field mark of the Moorhen.

The two long-billed rails are rather chickenlike in shape, and the diminutive Sora has a short, stubby bill. All have one thing in common: They skulk in dense reed beds of both salt- and freshwater marshes and are usually difficult to see well.

Plate 45—**Cormorants, Pelicans**

The three species of cormorants in our area are large, black goose-like birds in flight, but more loonlike when on the water, and like loons, they dive from the surface of the water. Cormorants have hooked bills but this feature is observed only at close range. When perched, they stand erect—often with their wings stretched out to dry. Unlike nearly all the other birds, cormorants do not possess waterproof feathers because they lack oil glands. During migration, cormorants are frequently seen flying overhead with steady wing-beats in very large numbers, either in long lines or in V-shaped flocks. Unlike geese, however, they are silent.

The pelicans, of which there are two kinds in our area, are famil-iar to all. One—the White Pelican—is mainly an inhabitant of inland freshwater, although it spends the winter months along the Gulf coast of Texas. The other one—the Brown Pelican—lives near the ocean, along the beaches. Lines of these prehistoric-looking birds alternately flap and glide in unison low over the surf. They plunge from moder-ate heights into the sea for fish, and often perch on posts, piers, and even fishing boats. Unlike the Brown Pelican, the huge White Pelican fishes from the surface in shallow waters. In flight, these spectacular birds, with gleaming white plumage and partially jet black wings, also alternately flap and sail in unison, sometimes in large flocks.

Plates 46 and 47—**Long-legged Waders**

Herons are wading birds whose habitat is often the best clue to their identification. They can usually be seen picking their way slowly through shallow water in marshes or along mudflats searching for fish, frogs, and other aquatic forms of life. They may also be observed roosting together in large numbers in trees and bushes near water where they breed. They may have either long or short legs and long or short necks, but they all have long bills, except for the field-inhabiting, insect-eating Cattle Egret and the seminoctur-nal Black-crowned Night-Heron.

The various white forms known as egrets, of which there are three species in our area, are members of this family (Great, Snowy, and the Cattle Egrets). People often confuse egrets and herons. All egrets are herons, but the reverse is not true—all herons are *not* egrets.

As for the Cattle Egret, this immigrant from Africa has spread far and wide and has become established over much of the United

States, although it is somewhat local in the West. Cattle Egrets feed on various insects that are flushed from the grass by moving cattle, other livestock, and farm tractors.

Unlike other herons, the American Bittern is solitary and reluctant to fly. For safety it relies on its cryptic pattern and coloration; as it stands motionless, its streaked breast blends in with the reeds. Although often skulking in marsh grass, chiefly cattails but also the giant reed (*Phragmites*), the diminutive Least Bittern may be seen in short flights, skimming just above the top of the marsh, or more rarely observed grasping cattail stems and even climbing among them.

Many people mistake herons for cranes. Cranes differ from the superficially similar but unrelated herons, particularly when in flight. Unlike herons, cranes fly with necks outstretched and in a V formation, or in long lines, like geese; they also flap and glide. Herons, on the other hand, fly with necks kinked or folded in, and with slow, steady wingbeats in loose flocks. The common crane in our area is the gray-colored Sandhill Crane.

As for the White-faced Ibis, the slender, decurved bill of this bird separates it immediately from all the other straight-billed species on these two plates.

Plates 48 to 52—**Shorebirds**

The shorebirds—or "waders," as they are sometimes called—frequent the shores of lakes and rivers and the edges of marshes, as well as tidal flats and ocean beaches. They reflect a diversity of types, which is matched by their many different names. There are two major subdivisions, based primarily on bill shapes that are adaptations for feeding: (1) the plovers, with short, stubby bills and (2) the sandpipers and allies, with long, slender bills. In addition, the following names are used in this very large and diversified group: oystercatcher, stilt, avocet, godwit, curlew, whimbrel, willet, yellowlegs, dowitcher, knot, turnstone, snipe, dunlin, and phalarope, plus two strictly Pacific Coast shorebirds—surfbird and tattler.

One of the first things to look for in a shorebird is the length and shape of the bill. For example, oystercatchers have laterally compressed, knifelike bills for opening and extracting shellfish; avocets and godwits have upturned bills; curlews and whimbrels have downturned ones; dowitchers and snipes have long, straight, slender bills for probing deep into the mud and ooze; stilts, willets, yellowlegs, and many sandpipers have long, needlelike bills for feeding in deep water and for picking up aquatic insects and marine forms; finally, plovers have shorter bills for picking up snails and other small types of animal life directly from the ground or from shallow pools, mud-flats, and sand beaches.

Plates 53 and 54—**Gulls, Terns**
The most numerous and familiar whitish or grayish birds seen perched or flying at the seashore or near lakes and other bodies of water are the gulls, which scavenge scraps from refuse dumps and parking lots. Several features distinguish gulls from their relatives, the terns. Gulls are usually, but not always, larger than terns. Gull bills are mostly heavier and slightly hooked at the tip, whereas those of terns are pointed. Gulls keep their bills pointed straight ahead when in flight, while terns keep their pointed downward. Gulls pick up their food on land or from the surface of the water, and they never dive. Terns dive headfirst into the water for fish.

Terns generally are more graceful looking, especially on the wing. Many species have forked tails and distinctive black caps, the larger species with slight crests. Several of the smaller gulls have black hoods in spring and summer, but the medium-sized and larger gulls are white headed the year round. Young gulls are mottled with gray; they are uniformly brownish when very young. A glance at these two plates will enable the reader to distinguish between the groups.

Attracting Birds

The sport and hobby of birding have grown over the years; so too has the use of bird feeders. They not only bring more species to the backyard but they also help the birds themselves, especially in colder areas where snow and ice may cover up their food. In retrospect, it can be seen that feeders have been an important factor in the rapid spread of some species (for example, the Northern Cardinal) to areas where they had been rare or even unknown. As conservation has become of widespread interest to millions, so too has increased awareness of the need to protect and aid birds. As a result, setting out feeders and gardening with an eye to attracting birds have become national pastimes. It is obvious that the greater the variety of birds, the greater the enjoyment of backyard birding.

Getting actively involved in feeding birds requires selecting feeders, setting them up in the right locations, and filling them with a good mixture of food.

Feeders

Feeders may be purchased in hardware stores, garden centers, nurseries, pet shops, and supermarkets. They range from simple feeders to elaborate bird "cafeterias." In selecting a feeder, remember that all you want is something to hold the food; it does not have to be complicated. Avoid metal feeders, which heat up in the summer sun and become tacky in freezing weather.

Feeders can be easily fashioned out of common objects found around the house. A plastic bleach bottle, for example, can be converted into a feeder, as can milk cartons, shoe boxes, and small wooden crates. Containers in which doors and windows have been cut can be suspended from a tree with metal coat hangers. A flat board with a raised edge around it to keep the seeds from spilling over also makes and efficient feeder. A shallow candy box on your bedroom window sill can serve as an alarm clock, as chirping birds are quite regular—and noisy—when clamoring for food early in the morning.

Store-bought feeders come in all sizes, shapes, and materials. Some are made of redwood and have glass sides and a shelf for food. Others look like plastic bubbles and can be hung up almost anywhere. There are also seed silos, post feeders, hummingbird feeders, and even small transparent boxes that can be attached to the windowpane with a suction cup. Many feeders dole out the seeds a little at a time, avoiding spillage and protecting the food from inclement weather.

We have just been talking about feeders used primarily for seed. Feeder use is not confined to seed eaters, however. Many also have suet racks for insect-eating birds, such as woodpeckers and nuthatches. Metal racks may even be nailed directly onto the tree trunk. Mesh bags (the kind that hold onions and oranges) may be filled with chunks of suet and suspended from a hook or branch. Be sure that the bags swing freely, otherwise aggressive European Starlings, which don't like the motion, will take over. The suet and fat should be discontinued in warm weather because they melt or become rancid.

Nectar-feeding birds, such as hummingbirds, will frequent a garden; watch such flowers as trumpet vine, petunias, salvia, or jewelweed. Hummers are especially attracted to red and orange colors. A hummingbird feeder filled with sugar water and a little red tape or paint on the bottle is another way to lure these birds into your yard.

Before putting a feeder into operation, be sure that its location is right. The ideal place is out of the wind, near natural cover, in an area that is sunny in winter and shady in summer. A kitchen window is frequently the perfect place. The ability to see the feeder from the house is the first prerequisite. Next, you want to see the *birds* in it, not squirrels. The feeder should be set up where squirrels cannot decimate the food supply and where cats cannot decimate the bird supply. Squirrels are very acrobatic. Consequently, baffles above and below feeders are necessary to keep them out, and the feeders must be away from trees and bushes so that the squirrels cannot leap into them. Once the station is working, food should not be placed on the ground, where a preoccupied bird can become easy prey of a cat. This is not to say that birds, on their own, won't feed on the ground; many do, but at least you won't be responsible for any mishap that might occur. To keep Rock Pigeons away, enclosures can be made with wire mesh large enough for small birds but too small for Rock Pigeons.

Now that the feeder is ready, what kind of seed should you get? Many commercial mixes of wild bird feed include large amounts of milo (round red seeds) or buckwheat, oats, and wheat, all of which you will find left behind in the feeder. Your best bet is sunflower seed, the favorite of Northern Cardinals, grosbeaks, chickadees, titmice, finches, and jays. For smaller seed-eating birds, white and red millet and cracked corn are popular. A number of birds favor peanut hearts, but this feed is also very attractive to starlings, which can quickly become pests. If you would like to try for goldfinches, Pine Siskins, and Purple Finches, thistle seed (also called niger seed) is sure to do the trick.

Many table scraps are also good for enticing birds, as are stale dry cereals, doughnuts, crackers and bread (especially favored by black-birds), and fruit—grapes, cherries, apples, oranges, and bananas for Mockingbirds and orioles. Near the shore and at ponds, bread will be gobbled up by gulls and ducks.

After choosing a feeder (or more than one, to attract a larger variety of birds), you must decide when to start using it. Wintertime in the colder areas is the essential period for feeding birds; do not stop until mild weather sets in.

It takes time to establish a feeder. You have to be patient and wait for birds to discover it. Unless birds are hard-pressed for food, they are likely to go beetle grubbing or seed gathering in an empty lot as to visit a feeder. Bad weather and a shortage of food, however, will bring them to you; lured by an easily available supply of their favorite foods. The variety of birds that come to feeders will depend on the variety of food put out. In warmer regions, the feeding station is more fun for the birder than a necessity for the birds. In colder areas, you must keep in mind that once a feeding station has been estab-lished in the fall, many birds become dependent on it. So don't start a feeding program if you are going to be away in the midwinter months and will be leaving the feeder untended.

Once the feeding routine has become established, birds will con-tinue as steady customers until spring, when buds, berries, and bugs are plentiful. At this time, put out some yarn, cotton, and strips of paper for nest-building birds.

If feeding is prolonged into the summer, adult birds may bring their young to the feeder, and eventually the young will come by themselves. Remember that young birds are unwary and easily caught by cats. If you continue to feed birds, you must make sure that cats don't come for a free meal too. To keep cats from pouncing out of the shrubs, a low metal or chicken-wire fence should be installed at the edge of flower borders, particularly thick borders (lily and iris beds), which are favorite hideouts for cats.

Birds Attracted by Food Type

	Seeds	Suet	Nectar	Grasses, Fruiting Shrubs, and Trees
Allen's Hummingbird			•	
American Crow	•	•		•
American Goldfinch	•			•
American (Black-billed) Magpie	•	•		•
American Robin	•			•
American Tree Swallow				•
Anna's Hummingbird			•	
Band-tailed Pigeon	•			•
Bewick's Wren	•	•		•
Black-capped Chickadee	•	•		•
Blue Jay	•	•		•
Bohemian Waxwing				•
Brewer's Blackbird	•			•
Broad-billed Hummingbird			•	
Broad-tailed Hummingbird			•	
Bronzed Cowbird	•			•
Brown Creeper	•	•		•
Brown-headed Cowbird	•			•
Bullock's Oriole			•	•
Bushtit	•	•		•
Cactus Wren	•	•		•
California (Brown) Towhee	•			•
California Quail	•			•
Calliope Hummingbird			•	
Cedar Waxwing				•
Chestnut-backed Chickadee	•	•		•
Chipping Sparrow	•			•
Common Grackle	•	•		
Common Raven	•	•		
Common Yellowthroat				•
Costa's Hummingbird			•	
Curve-billed Thrasher	•	•		•

	Seeds	Suet	Nectar	Grasses, Fruiting Shrubs, and Trees
Dark-eyed Junco	•	•		•
Downy Woodpecker	•	•		•
European Starling	•	•		•
Evening Grosbeak	•	•		•
Fox Sparrow	•	•		•
Gambel's Quail	•			•
Gila Woodpecker			•	•
Golden-crowned Sparrow	•			•
Gray Catbird	•			•
Gray-crowned Rosy-Finch	•			
Gray Jay	•	•		•
Great-tailed Grackle	•			
Hairy Woodpecker	•	•		•
Harris's Sparrow	•			•
Hepatic Tanager			•	•
Hooded Oriole			•	•
House Finch	•			•
House Sparrow	•			•
House Wren		•		•
Inca Dove	•			•
Lawrence's Goldfinch	•			•
Lesser (Green-backed) Goldfinch	•			•
Mountain Chickadee	•	•		•
Mourning Dove	•			•
Northern Bobwhite	•			•
Northern Cardinal	•			•
Northern Flicker	•	•		•
Northern Mockingbird	•			•
Nuttall's Woodpecker		•		•
Oak (Plain) Titmouse	•	•		•
Pileated Woodpecker		•		•
Pine Grosbeak	•			•
Pine Siskin	•	•		•
Pinyon Jay	•	•		•

	Seeds	Suet	Nectar	Grasses, Fruiting Shrubs, and Trees
Purple Finch	●	●		●
Pygmy Nuthatch	●	●		●
Pyrrhuloxia	●			●
Red-breasted Nuthatch	●	●		●
Red-eyed Vireo				●
Red-winged Blackbird	●	●		●
Ring-necked Pheasant	●			●
Rock (Dove) Pigeon	●			●
Ruby-crowned Kinglet	●	●		●
Rufous Hummingbird			●	
Scott's Oriole			●	●
Song Sparrow	●			●
Spotted Towhee	●			●
Steller's Jay	●	●		●
Summer Tanager			●	●
Tree Sparrow	●			●
Western Scrub-Jay	●	●		●
Western Tanager			●	●
White-breasted Nuthatch	●	●		●
White-crowned Sparrow	●			●
White-throated Sparrow	●			●
Wild Turkey	●			●
Yellow-billed Cuckoo				●
Yellow-breasted Chat		●		●
Yellow Warbler				●

Water

Water is as much a part of a feeding station as food. Winter and summer, birds need drinking water. Some birds will also bathe, even on bitterly cold days. Heating mechanisms may be installed in birdbaths to keep them from freezing. In summer, on hot dry days, an oscillating lawn sprinkler will bring birds down from the treetops—small birds, such as warblers and kinglets, that you never suspected were around will turn up. An old leaking bucket filled with water and dripping into a pan will serve the same purpose.

Nest Boxes

In addition to creating a sanctuary for birds with feeders, birdbaths, landscaping, and food, nest boxes can be provided for breeding birds. In bluebird country, for example, there is intense competition between other hole-nesting birds and shy native bluebirds, which give way to aggressive European Starlings and House Sparrows. Entrance holes should be small enough for the bluebird, alone. Tree Swallows might move into a bluebird house, but they are welcome guests. Just put out more houses, and there will be plenty of room for all. An open area without trees, not far from water, is a perfect site for a Purple Martin house. In return for the lodging, the birds will feast on mosquitoes and other noxious insects.

Shrubs and Trees

Landscaping for food and shelter is a necessity for a successful feeding station. Geographic location and local climate will influence the selection of plants. The planting of shrubs and trees may seem an overwhelming task, but nature will help if given a chance. Frequently, seedlings will pop up among the bushes from a stray seed or from bird droppings.

Deciduous and evergreen shrubs, trees, and vines should be planted for their buds, fruits, or seeds. Avoid plants known as nonnative invasives. Several desirable species are listed at the end of this chapter. Many deciduous trees are easy to plant, and in early spring they produce buds, flowers and foliage that attract insect-eating birds. Alders, birches, and poplars also produce catkins, which provide seeds for later consumption. Cherry trees can be transplanted from the wild or might just appear from a stray seed dropped by a bird.

Aside from organized gardening, there are a number of miscellaneous suggestions that might be helpful. Thick, unrestrained shrubbery will provide good cover as well as nesting and roosting sites. A discarded Christmas tree set up in the yard makes a good windbreak and shelter for birds. A wild corner given over to bittersweet, catbrier, chokeberry, and pokeberry will become an impenetrable tangle appealing to nesting Spotted Towhees and other thicket-haunting birds. Incidentally, dead trees or limbs should be left for woodpeckers. If a utility wire runs through your property, watch it for perching flycatchers or migrating swallows. A well-trimmed lawn attracts American Robins and ant-pursuing Northern Flickers. The base of a privet hedge adjacent to an open lawn may be preferred by thrushes, sparrows, and buntings.

Some Deciduous and Evergreen Trees, Shrubs, and Vines That Should Be Planted for Their Buds, Fruits, or Seeds

Alder	Elm
Ash	Fir
Aspen	Grape (Wild)
Bayberry	Hackberry
Beech	Hawthorn
Birch	Hemlock
Bittersweet	Huckleberry
Blackberry	Huisache
Blueberry	Maple
Box Elder	Mountain Ash
Catbrier	Mulberry
Cedar	Oak
Cherry	Peach
Chokeberry	Pecan
Cottonwood	Persimmon
Crab Apple	Pine
Currant	Pokeberry
Cypress (Cedar)	Privet
Dogwood	Raspberry
Elderberry	Red Cedar

Sassafras

Serviceberry (Western Shadbush)

Sour Gum (Tupelo)

Spicebush

Spruce

Sumac

Sweet Gum

Sycamore

Tamarack

Toyon

Viburnum

Walnut

Willow

Yew

Flowers That Attract Hummingbirds

Acacia

Aloe

Barrel Cactus

Beardtongue

Bee Balm

Bergamot

Cardinal Flower

Century Plant

Cholla Cactus

Columbine

Coral Bells

Creosote Bush

Fuchsia

Geranium

Hibiscus

Hollyhock

Indian Paintbrush

Jewelweed

Jimsonweed

Lantana

Larkspur

Locust

Morning Glory

Nasturtium

Ocotillo

Paloverde

Petunia

Phlox

Redbud

Redhot Poker

Saguaro Cactus

Salvia

Spanish Bayonet

Thistle

Trumpet Vine

Appendix A: Optical Equipment

Whether at home or away, one can watch birds with the naked eye, but to identify them correctly and to study them well some optical equipment is essential. At first, perhaps, 2- to 3-power opera glasses might suffice, but in order to bring a bird up close enough to observe fine details, a pair of prism binoculars is a must.

Start with a lightweight pair, the magnification of which should be no more than 7 to 8 power; that is, the bird under observation should appear at least seven times closer than if viewed without binoculars. Binoculars that are either 7 x 35, or, even better, 7 x 50 are undoubtedly the best. Binoculars more powerful than 7 or 8 will be heavier and more cumbersome to use. Remember—the figure after the x represents the amount of light; 50 is better than 35.

Be certain that the binoculars you buy have a central focus, that is, a wheel or other device in the center to turn or focus both lenses quickly and at the same time. This feature is most important, especially for viewing moving birds, for which instant focusing is imperative.

When purchasing optical equipment, make sure that the lenses are clear and that no distortions are present. Do *not* buy binoculars until you have looked through them. They must be in perfect order in every respect, including proper alignment, so as not to strain your eyes.

For those birds that are seen at a distance, such as waterfowl on the other side of a large lake or perhaps a hawk on a high cliff, something more powerful is needed. Especially useful is a telescope mounted on a tripod. The scope should range anywhere from 10 to 20 power and, preferably, should have a zoom lens for quick results. In telescopes of higher power, vibration and atmospheric interference can blur the image; therefore, anything stronger than 20 power is not recommended. Furthermore, the objective may be blurred because of heat haze or merely less light, causing less sharpness.

Also necessary is a lightweight tripod on which to mount the telescope. Be sure that the legs have clamps that press down to make them more secure. *Never* buy a tripod that has leg screws. Sand and grit will get into the threads, and constant loosening and tightening will cause the joints to become threadbare.

Appendix B: Glossary

Barred: crosswise *horizontal* markings, as in tails of many hawks

Breeding: spring, summer—periods or plumages

Decurved: downward curved bill

Facial disk: rounded front part of face, as in owls

Frontal shield: bare covering at base of bill, as in gallinules

Head tuft: clump of feathers on top of head, as in some owls and Horned Lark

Lobed: partially webbed

Lore: space between bill and eye

Mandibles: upper and lower bills

Median line: stripe through center of crown

Nape: back of neck

Nonbreeding: fall, winter—periods or plumages

Primaries: long flight feathers of outer wing

Rectrices: tail feathers

Rump: lower back just above tail

Secondaries: long flight feathers of inner wing

Semipalmated: partially webbed

Serrated: "toothed" bill edge, as in mergansers

Spectacle: eye ring, with connecting streak through lore

Streaked: lengthwise markings, as in many sparrows

Tarsus: the generally exposed "shin" part of leg

Vent: undertail feather groups

Vermiculated: fine, wavy, lateral streaks on feathers

Index

Cowbird, Brown-headed *(Molothrus ater)*, 46

Crane, Sandhill *(Grus canadensis)*, 100

Creeper, Brown *(Certhia americana)*, 50

Crossbill, Red *(Loxia curvirostra)*, 10

Crossbill, White-winged *(Loxia leucoptera)*, 10

Crow, American *(Corvus brachyrhynchos)*, 48

Cuckoo, Yellow-billed *(Coccyzus americanus)*, 62

Curlew, Long-billed *(Numenius americanus)*, 104

Dickcissel *(Spiza americana)*, 44

Dipper, American *(Cinclus mexicanus)*, 24

Dove, Common Ground- *(Columbina passerina)*, 62

Dove, Inca *(Columbina inca)*, 62

Dove, Mourning *(Zenaida macroura)*, 62

Dove, Spotted *(Streptopelia chinensis)*, 62

Dove, White-winged *(Zenaida asiatica)*, 62

Dowitcher, Long-billed *(Limnodromus scolopaceus)*, 106

Duck, Black-bellied Whistling- *(Dendrocygna autumnalis)*, 82

Duck, Fulvous Whistling- *(Dendrocygna bicolor)*, 82

Duck, Harlequin *(Histrionicus histrionicus)*, 90

Duck, Ring-necked *(Aythya collaris)*, 86

Duck, Ruddy *(Oxyura jamaicensis)*, 90

Duck, Wood *(Aix sponsa)*, 84

Dunlin *(Calidris alpina)*, 108

Eagle, Bald *(Haliaeetus leucocephalus)*, 68

Eagle, Golden *(Aquila chrysaetos)*, 68

Egret, Cattle *(Bubulcus ibis)*, 100

Egret, Great *(Ardea alba)*, 100

Egret, Snowy *(Egretta thula)*, 100

Falcon, Peregrine *(Falco peregrinus)*, 74

Falcon, Prairie *(Falco mexicanus)*, 74

Finch, Gray-crowned Rosy- *(Leucosticte tephrocotis)*, 10

Finch, House *(Carpodacus mexicanus)*, 10

Finch, Purple *(Carpodacus purpureus)*, 10

Flicker, Northern *(Colaptes auratus)*, 52

Flycatcher, Ash-throated *(Myiarchus cinerascens)*, 22

Quail, Mountain *(Oreotyx pictus)*, 64
Quail, Scaled *(Callipepla squamata)*, 64

Rail, Clapper *(Rallus longirostris)*, 96
Rail, Virginia *(Rallus limicola)*, 96
Raven, Common *(Corvus corax)*, 48
Redhead *(Aytha americana)*, 86
Redstart, American *(Setophaga ruticilla)*, 18
Redstart, Painted *(Myioborus pictus)*, 18
Roadrunner, Greater *(Geococcyx californianus)*, 66
Robin, American *(Turdus migratorius)*, 42
Rosy-Finch, Gray-crowned *(Leucosticte tephrocotis)*, 10

Sage-Grouse, Greater *(Centrocercus urophasianus)*, 66
Sanderling *(Calidris alba)*, 108
Sandpiper, Least *(Calidris minutilla)*, 108
Sandpiper, Rock *(Calidris ptilocnemis)*, 110
Sandpiper, Spotted *(Actitis macularius)*, 106
Sandpiper, Upland *(Bartramia longicauda)*, 106
Sandpiper, Western *(Calidris mauri)*, 108
Sapsucker, Red-breasted *(Sphyrapicus ruber)*, 52
Sapsucker, Red-naped (Yellow-bellied) *(Sphyrapicus nuchalis)*, 52
Sapsucker, Williamson's *(Sphyrapicus thyroideus)*, 52
Scaup, Greater *(Aythya marila)*, 86
Scaup, Lesser *(Aythya affinis)*, 86
Scoter, Black *(Melanitta nigra)*, 90
Scoter, Surf *(Melanitta perspicillata)*, 90
Scoter, White-winged *(Melanitta fusca)*, 90
Screech-Owl, Western *(Otus kennicottii)*, 76
Scrub-Jay, Western *(Aphelocoma californica)*, 28
Shoveler, Northern *(Ana clypeata)*, 84
Shrike, Loggerhead *(Lanius ludovicianus)*, 24
Siskin, Pine *(Carduelis pinus)*, 14
Snipe, Common *(Gallinago gallinago)*, 106
Solitaire, Townsend's *(Myadestes townsendi)*, 24
Sora *(Porzana carolina)*, 96
Sparrow, Black-chinned *(Spizella atrogularis)*, 32
Sparrow, Black-throated *(Amphispiza bilineata)*, 32